A CHRISTIAN SURVIVAL GUIDE

A CHRISTIAN SURVIVAL GUIDE

A LIFELINE TO FAITH AND GROWTH

ED CYZEWSKI

Kregel
Publications

A Christian Survival Guide: A Lifeline to Faith and Growth
© 2014 by Ed Cyzewski

Published by Kregel Publications, a division of Kregel, Inc., 2450 Oak Industrial Drive NE, Grand Rapids, MI 49505.

Published in association with the literary agency of Credo Communications, LLC, Grand Rapids, Michigan, www.credocommunications.net.

To protect the privacy of some individuals mentioned in this book, names and identifying details have been changed.

ISBN 978-0-8254-4331-2

Printed in the United States of America
14 15 16 17 18 / 5 4 3 2 1

*To my in-laws, John and Alta Ludlam, who
are responsible for the survival of my faith
when answers failed me.*

CONTENTS

ACKNOWLEDGMENTS

No writer can accomplish much of anything without a lot of support. I am deeply indebted to my wife, Julie, who patiently picked up after me and offered unwavering encouragement as I hit the home stretch of this book. Julie has offered immensely helpful feedback and encouraged me to keep working on this project. I would never have finished this book without your support, Julie. I'm also deeply grateful to our son, Ethan, for taking longer naps, cheerfully playing while I worked, and sleeping like a champ at night. My parents provided critical childcare support along the way.

I'm grateful for the staff at Kregel as we developed this project. Dennis Hillman, Steve Barclift, and the rest of the editorial team provided helpful feedback and guidance throughout. Paul Brinkerhoff distinguished himself as a thoughtful, insightful, and skilled editor who mended paragraphs with precision and suggested additions that always improved the book. I'm indebted to him for his feedback that pushed me to write better and his additions that brought clarity. Noelle Pedersen kept the production and publicity on track with a steady stream of updates and prompt replies to every email. My agent, Karen Neumair, continues to amaze me with her support, organization, and professionalism. It's also nice to have an agent who likes to swap gardening ideas.

My pastors were instrumental in the development of my ideas over the years: Vince Geier, Jeff Cannell, Jared Boyd, and Mark Willey.

My friends Emma Liddle, Thomas Turner, and Heather A. Goodman provided important feedback on early drafts. Alise Wright, Jeff Cannell, Kelly J. Youngblood, Randall Payleitner, Tammy Perlmutter, Toni Hollopeter, Trip Kimball, John Nunnikhoven, Tanya Marlow, Matthew Paul Turner, Kelly Arabie, Jean Purcell, Derek Cooper, and Tyler Yoder provided feedback on a variety of chapters and helped to make this book so much better. The readers of my blogs (www.inamirrordimly.com and www.edcyzewski.com) have been an ongoing source of encouragement and insight. I'm sure I've overlooked others who have improved this project.

Of course the people I'm most grateful for are my friends both in real life and online who openly talked about their struggles with Christianity. I've written this book for you and I pray that the process of reading it is as much of a blessing for you as it was for me to write.

INTRODUCTION

FROM SURVIVING TO THRIVING

KING SAUL WASN'T THE guy you'd want to join on a road trip. Violent without his favorite songs and opposed to stopping for snacks, he would've tried the patience of Job. Once, his choice of a rest stop almost cost him his life.

Jealous of his servant David's military success and popular support, Saul began chasing him throughout the land of Judah. While running from Saul, David often linked his survival to the remote fresh springs of En Gedi along the Dead Sea coast. En Gedi also had a series of caves that made it an ideal location for a fugitive.

When he least expected it, David had an opportunity to secure his own survival. Unaware that David and his men were hiding in the back of the cave, Saul stepped in to relieve himself. With sword in hand, David waited for him.

However, as a man tuned in to the will of God, David resisted the opportunity to kill the king. Saul was God's anointed king, and David recognized that killing Saul to survive today would bring disastrous consequences tomorrow. Though David knew how to survive as a soldier, he also knew how to survive as a servant of God. Killing God's anointed king was an obvious sin that he could not commit.

Righteous as David appears in this scene, he couldn't resist a good

11

prank. I love him for this. While Saul relieved himself, David cut off a piece of his clothing. After Saul left the cave, David walked out and waved it at Saul and his company of soldiers.

I can't believe the boldness of David in this story. He was most likely outnumbered, and all of his men were trapped in a cave. If Saul so desired, he could have sent his men in to kill them all. However, Saul, at least in this case, realized that he'd been wrong to pursue David. Conceding that David was more righteous, he called off the hunt.

David placed himself at the mercy of God in that situation. He committed himself to obeying the will of God, assuring his spiritual survival even if it put his physical survival in danger. In the end, God honored David's commitment to holiness and preserved his life in the process.

SURVIVAL IS NOT A MISTAKE

Survival requires planning. What if we expected survival in the woods to happen without planning ahead?

"I'm sure I'll be able to figure out which mushrooms and berries to eat. Pine cones are nature's waffles."

"Anyone can start a fire by rubbing two sticks together. Tom Hanks did it in *Cast Away*."

"Don't they use fresh stream water to brew beer? Of course I can drink it."

"What's wrong with hiding under a tree in a thunderstorm?"

"I have the food situation covered. I can just spear fish. Did I mention that I've seen *Cast Away*?"

"I read that Chris Farley Mowat book in grade school, so I've got the wolf situation covered."

"If I find a baby bear, I'm sure its mother won't mind if I give it a big 'bear hug.'"

Choosing the right path to personal and spiritual survival was not easy or necessarily obvious. David's men thought that God had delivered Saul into his hands, but David would not let them tempt him. How did David manage to make such a cool-headed, God-honoring decision when conventional wisdom pointed to the opposite course of action? At the very least, he was prepared for survival as a follower of God when a tough situation came his way.

If David wasn't prepared to resist temptation while hiding in the cave, we wouldn't read about his kingship or his many psalms, making for a much shorter Old Testament and one less class for seminary students. Our survival as followers of Jesus may hinge on our preparations for the decisions we make and the challenges we face. David resisted killing Saul because he'd committed himself to learning the will of God and acting on it. Whether we need to cultivate specific disciplines, learn how to resist temptation, or address the nagging doubts in our lives, Christian survival doesn't just happen. It requires discipline, planning, and action. If we fail to prepare, we may fall short of God's best and even put the survival of our faith in jeopardy.

In fact, the path to "survival" isn't just a matter of doing the bare minimum to survive. When temptation hits or a dark season arrives in our lives, a flimsy faith and tacked on spiritual practices won't provide the sturdy support we need. Christian survival demands that we face the challenges to our faith and learn to rest daily in Christ, our solid foundation.

Christians who neglect their spiritual growth, the actions God calls them to take, and the teachings that ground their faith are setting themselves up for failure. Perhaps they may never fall away from God, but Jesus talked about having abundant spiritual life like a bubbling spring, not squeaking by with a Sunday morning attendance card. If the same old doubts linger or the same old sins show up at confession time, I'd suggest that it's time to take care of them before they hurt you, the people you love, and your relationship with God. In addition, we could be blindsided with tough situations or questions that disrupt what we thought to be true. There are few things more disruptive for our faith than the unexpected loss of a long-held belief. No one ever plans to fail in the Christian faith, but we do prepare ourselves for failure through neglect, just as we can prepare ourselves for survival by taking action.

When I speak of Christian survival, I'm talking about the real problems and doubts that can hinder your relationship with Jesus and your fellowship with others. In America we are bombarded with all kinds of campaigns, organizations, and agendas that are supposed to be important to us as Christians. We're told by politicians on both sides that we need to support legislation that will preserve the "moral character" of America. We learn that our country is either in danger of being taken over by maniacal socialists/fascists (which is an impossible mix by the way) who will turn America into Canada or that fundamentalists will turn our open-minded republic into the Holy Land Experience. Others warn us that men need to watch ultimate fighting or they'll start baking cupcakes and give up their careers to stay home with the kids, and that women need to raise kids and bake cupcakes lest they spend their free time watching ultimate fighting.

We are bombarded by campaigns to build museums that tout certain agendas or prove certain views of the Bible. Some lament that America is on the brink of becoming a land crawling with atheists and therefore we need to buy a certain book, attend another conference, or believe some checklist of absolutes. Others fear that America is on the brink of being overrun with religious zealots who want to take control of the minute details of our lives.

I trust that the people behind such campaigns mean well and that they love Jesus, but these "important" issues are not *essential* for our faith as Christians. I'm far more concerned about getting the basics of Christianity right: learning how to pray regularly, how to commune with the Holy Spirit, how to love our neighbors, and how to read the Bible so that we can live in relationship with Christ and do God's will on earth. If the basics are following Jesus, loving God, and loving others, shouldn't we make our top priority the removal of all potential obstacles that could keep us from God?

In addition, there are some vocal critics of Christianity who claim it has failed them and that the Jesus we know was invented by clever storytellers. They bring tough questions that demand answers. Have you ever listened to someone who left the faith? Former Christians can often bring up the kinds of survival issues we need to consider.

I once worked with this guy who was a smart, well-read, committed agnostic. He'd converted to Christianity in college and later served as a Campus Crusade leader and a small group Bible study facilitator in his church. While he never shared the specifics, at a certain point he gave up on God. It stopped clicking for him. I'll be honest, I was afraid to even ask. It was "better" to just think I was smarter or more holy than him rather than learn about his crisis of faith. Isn't that always easier?

This situation left me perplexed. How could I relate with this colleague? My training in Christianity taught me to present the facts of the gospel, but if he already had the information, what more could I offer him? Especially if he knew everything I did and still didn't believe. How could I say anything different to change his mind?

My relationship with this agnostic colleague caused me to think deeply about my own attitude and behavior at work, especially when our personalities clashed. I had to move beyond my reliance on the right answers in order to figure out not only how to embody the gospel message but also why we were different. We both had the same information, so where did he fall off the tracks? What enables some to survive as Christians when others have faltered?

This book aims to help the saints persevere, and so we'll focus on answering that last question—what will help you survive as a follower of Jesus?

Surviving as a Christian depends on having the right beliefs, putting them into practice in community with other Christians, and most importantly, meeting with God regularly. If we fail to address basic survival matters such as understanding God's story from Scripture, defeating sin, or living in step with the Holy Spirit, we run the risk of missing out on the abundant life Jesus promised us, if not losing our intimacy with Jesus and leaving the faith altogether.

Like David, we never know when a challenge to our faith will come our way. There's no guarantee that the people around us will lead us to the right decisions. We have to take responsibility for our survival as followers of Jesus.

A KNOW-IT-ALL WITH SIMPLE ANSWERS?

By putting together this survival guide to Christianity, I run a few risks. For starters, I could give the impression that I have my act completely together—like I'm some kind of Special Forces Christian who drags people through my personal boot camp in order to make them awesome and perfect—just . . . like . . . me. When sharing what God has done in my life, I know this is an easy mistake to make.

While I want to freely share what God has done in my life and what he has been teaching me about Christian survival, I don't want you to forget that I still skip my Bible reading some days, fail to focus when praying, make selfish mistakes in my marriage, and cheer for Philadelphia sports teams. I also rely on coffee to the point that I feel like it should be a sin. I've tried to make this guide feel like I'm sharing my own story and thoughts about following Jesus with you at a café and you've just bought me a drink—a really large light roast coffee with a lot of caffeine.

I come to this book as a lifelong Christian who has hit some rough patches and seasons of doubt that truly threatened my own faith. I learned to ask hard questions while attending seminary, and have written about many of them in print and online. Many of the topics in this book have been extremely hard for me to confront personally. In addition, I've often found that almost everyone I know has struggled with many of the topics I discuss in this book. They just keep coming up in one conversation after another. At some point I had to stop running from the hard questions and tough topics. The more I dreaded a topic, the more I knew I needed to deal with it. I didn't always end up with the range of answers I expected, but I have also met God in the places where I had the most uncertainty, shame, and weakness. I pray that you'll find the same hope as you confront your own questions and uncertainties.

Once I convince you that I'm Joe Christian, the other mistake I can make is to minimize the problems I confront in this book or present my solutions as pat, simple, or completely satisfactory. Throughout this book I'll aim to remain true to the difficulties and exceptions of life while dealing with truth, principles, and experiences that may prove helpful. I also want to give space for the range of Christian beliefs, practices, and experiences, offering a variety of options when appropriate. In addition, I've had to keep each chapter painfully short in order to cover so many topics, so keep in mind that I'm providing a simple overview that can be supplemented with further reading from the chapter-by-chapter "For Further Reading" list I've included at the end of the book. I may not be able to provide answers for your every problem, but I hope that I can help you take some solid steps forward.

It's my experience that many Christians tend to hit two extremes when talking about following Jesus. We either hide our tough questions and doubts behind a happy, faith-washed veneer, or we wallow in the complexity, difficulty, and messiness of our faith without actively seeking solutions that appear too pat or inauthentic.

Either way, we avoid our doubts and questions because they're either not appropriate for good Christians or only a jerk would dare to challenge messy Christians to confront their sins and doubts. These represent fine lines we'll try to walk. Sinners are most certainly welcome, but in the

SURVIVAL TIPS

The Messy Christian and the Happy Christian can both fail to thrive as followers of Jesus.

Marks of Messy Christians

- Believe God only dispenses grace and doesn't challenge us to clean up our acts.
- Hypersensitive to judgment.
- Despite doubts and struggles, they fail to consider possible steps forward.
- Uncomfortable with words such as "certainty" or "confidence."

Marks of Happy Christians

- Would rather go to the Wednesday evening service than admit they have doubts or struggles in their Christian faith and practice.
- Desire to appear certain and together. They fear accountability and confession, especially with those "self-righteous" people at church.
- Attack those who are too vocal about their doubts or the problems they find in Christianity. It's all in the name of "defending" the faith.

grand scheme of things, you're either moving into the kingdom or out of it. At some point you need to decide whether you're going to follow a convicted insurrectionist to his execution or your own plans. There is a way forward, and it is messy, but there is real progress we can make in our walk with God.

If you're on the losing side that will one day inherit the earth, then we'll have some tough eggs to crack. However, I firmly believe that God can handle our tough questions, doubts, and struggles. There are good, if not excellent, answers and perspectives to be found in the Christian faith. I'm not guaranteeing that the suggestions and answers in each chapter will be a custom fit to your life, but they'll give you a solid base for your survival plans. Rather than letting these matters of doubt and sin simmer and eventually boil over, I suggest facing them directly.

Throughout each chapter we'll look at some common scenarios that illustrate a particular question or problem that may threaten the faith or growth of Christians. Once we're on the same page, we'll work our way through some possible solutions. Some answers or action plans will be more specific than others. For example, there are some fairly uniform steps that most Christians can take in developing good prayer and Bible study habits. However, when it comes to finding healthy Christian community, the possible solutions will vary. These chapters will offer several biblically based options even if there isn't a consensus among believers.

WE AREN'T SLACKERS FOR JESUS

While we're talking about the basics of Christian survival, I don't want to give the impression for one moment that our goal is to simply get by. In choosing to follow Jesus we are leaving the promises of this world behind for new life in his kingdom. We cannot serve two masters, and therefore we're either all in or all out. There is no in-between.

Therefore, by committing to our "survival" as Christians we are running the race with every intention of winning. Who takes marriage vows like, "I vow to do the bare minimum to prevent a divorce"? Sure, putting the toilet seat down, taking the kids out for ice cream, and buying the occasional bouquet are good things, but marriage is a full-scale commitment of yourself to another person. God's *agape* love didn't leave anything behind when Jesus hung on the cross. God's love is all in for me and for you. This is a love worth clinging to even when we can't make sense of a tragedy that befalls a loved one or a season of confusion and uncertainty.

As we talk about our commitment to Christian survival I encourage you to think in terms of deleting the numbers of old flames from your phone before getting married. These are things that all Christians need to consider in order to shore up their faith as they move forward. If left unresolved, problems with many of the issues discussed in this book will ruin your relationship with God down the line like a call from that old girlfriend while you and your wife are going through a rough time. Like those old numbers, our sins and unasked questions cannot remain. We

THE MILK AND MEAT OF CHRISTIAN MATURITY

With my apologies to vegans and vegetarians, Christian survival aims to help you "digest" or master the basics (the milk) of the faith so you can know God better (the meat) and produce fruit. That metaphor breaks down somewhere between the meat and the fruit, but we can at least agree that fruit is good—even if it's coming from meat. Paul describes Christian maturity as milk and meat in 1 Corinthians 3:2: "I gave you milk, not solid food, for you were not yet ready for it. Indeed, you are still not ready."

Christians Who Need Milk

- Are worldly, not living by the Spirit
- Quarrel
- Divide into factions, overemphasizing loyalty to leaders
- Serve by their own strength
- Are deceived, thinking of themselves as wise

Christians Ready for Meat

- Live in the Spirit's power
- Resolve disputes
- Reach unity in the Spirit
- Rely on the Spirit's wisdom

are preparing ourselves for a lifetime commitment to God, and therefore we need to confront our doubts and work on the basics of following Jesus before moving on to the deeper spiritual life that God has for us.

And speaking of basics, let's keep in mind that our goal in mastering these basics of Christian survival is continued growth as faithful disciples of Jesus. If you learned how to play T-ball when you were five, you probably learned how to swing a bat and throw a ball even though you weren't turning double plays. You may have had some basic skills back then, but can you imagine a group of adults getting together to play some T-ball? T-ball was a necessary step in the development of many baseball and softball players, but we are expected to build on what we learn and to develop new skills. When a professional player struggles to hit the ball, he may use a tee to work on his swing, but returning to the tee is only a temporary part of his long-term training as a hitter.

Paul spoke in terms of milk and meat when addressing the Corinthians about their spiritual growth. As they stumbled into sin over and over again, they required the basic milk of the gospel to remind them that they were free from sin. As they persisted in bickering and fighting, letting sin run rampant among them, they could not mature in their relationships with God and in their dealings with one another until they digested the milk of the gospel.

This Christian survival guide provides both milk and meat that together aim to aid disciples of Jesus in their overall spiritual growth. Some topics may strike you as more relevant than others, but I encourage you to wrestle with all of them. Chances are that at some point you will run into someone who is struggling with that very thing, and then you'll be prepared to help. At one time or another I have either personally experienced difficulties with each topic addressed or spoken with Christians and former Christians who found these matters difficult. There may be someone in your small group or family who needs your help with one of the topics covered in this survival guide.

As we move into our first survival topic, I pray that you will be guided by the Holy Spirit and encouraged as you face some tough questions and seek the answers God has for you. Our God is able.

PART 1

CHRISTIAN BELIEFS

PRAYER

A STILL SMALL VOICE FOR BIG LOUD PROBLEMS

TWO RADIO EXECUTIVES had been trailing Billy Graham as he preached at venues all across America in the 1950s. They wanted to sign Graham to a contract for a prime-time radio slot. The trouble was that Graham refused. Every time they found Graham's hotel, he would sneak out back doors and climb down fire escapes.

They finally caught up with Graham in Seattle, but they couldn't arrange a meeting. However, before the two execs boarded their flight, they received a message from Graham. Several business owners had offered to help pay for the radio program, and Graham decided to hear them out, even if he still needed to raise an additional $23,000 to make the radio show a reality.

After making their pitch to Graham, they watched Graham fall to his knees and entrust the radio ministry to the Lord. In fact, after praying earnestly about the radio show, Graham asked the Lord to send him the full $23,000 by midnight if it was God's will for him to move forward. While Graham didn't want to take away from his preaching ministry, he also believed that God could make a way for him.

That evening Graham collected donations for the radio show, but he fell short of his goal. Resolved to follow God's direction, Graham went to bed without signing the radio contract. However, before he turned out the lights, one of Graham's team members found three envelopes waiting for him at the hotel's front desk. They made up the remaining difference to pay for the show.

We could cite a lot of reasons for Graham's success, but Graham himself made no mistake about giving all of the credit to God. Each step he took had been guided by earnest prayer, seeking God's direction and only moving when he sensed the conviction of God. That didn't mean he was spared moments of doubt and struggle. If his ministry was going to endure, he would need to continue laying his cares before God.

We can all see that someone like Billy Graham really needed to pray while planning preaching tours or paying for a national radio show. Who wouldn't need prayer for stuff like that? However, this commitment to prayer was a key part of Graham's life long before he became a world-famous preacher. As a young man he often took long "prayer walks" to seek out the will of God. Graham no doubt modeled his approach to prayer on the example of Jesus.

Surprising though it may be, Jesus spent significant amounts of time praying. Wasn't Jesus already pretty tight with God since he was a member of the Trinity? The fact that he took time to pray is a Trinitarian brain bender. If Jesus made prayer an integral part of his life, what makes us think we can do any better without it? If anything, Jesus sent us a very important message about the practice and importance of prayer. Our survival as followers of Jesus depends on it. Since our Lord modeled prayer for us, we'd better figure out a place for it in our lives.

While a recent Pew Forum poll found that 78 percent of evangelicals pray daily,[1] "prayer" could mean any number of practices that could lead to a wide variety of different results. A "win the lottery" prayer is quite different from a "give us our daily bread" prayer. While I'm glad so many value prayer, let's talk about how to pray and how prayer can help us survive as followers of Jesus.

Many Christians I know today, myself included, struggle with a condition I call "prayer guilt." We all like to pray. We all see the value of prayer. We even pray most days. However, we always feel like we never pray enough. If we have prayed, we didn't pray long enough or failed to stay focused while praying. I'll tell myself, Sure I prayed, but the prayers weren't very good. It would be nice to at least have a vision or speak in a tongue or two before checking prayer off my "to do" list.

I've spent far too many days living with an underlying sense that I should be praying more or doing more for God. I can always think of someone who must be meditating longer, reciting prayers that are more ancient, or lighting taller, brighter candles. Whether or not I'm correct, that guilt leaves me feeling inadequate and unable to approach God with the kind of confidence that Jesus talks about.

The outcomes of prayer are so hard to quantify. On the one hand we read about people who can't imagine surviving a single day without beginning it on their knees before God. And then on the other we rush from one thing to another and lay in bed at night wondering where the day went. I've gone to bed in the past thinking, "Oops, I forgot to pray today."

ONE-WAY PRAYERS

When I started to take prayer seriously, I learned a way of praying that I call "freestyle prayer." The plan was pretty simple: bow your head and start talking to God. It was way more personal than many of the prayers I'd learned to recite while growing up.

On the one hand, it was awesome. I broke through many of the barriers that I'd felt between myself and God as I shared my problems just as I would with a friend. Of course, that also meant that I talked about myself and my problems a lot. I also used up my lifetime quota of the word "just." You know these prayers: "We just want to thank you for just providing for our every need so we can just keep praying just like this . . ."

During my youth I had used prayer as a tool for absolution, saying a pile of "Our Fathers" after confessing my sins to a priest, but the freestyle prayers I learned in a small country church sent me to the other extreme. If prayer was "talking *to* God," I certainly had no problem controlling the conversation. I remember marveling that Jesus could spend an entire evening praying. I wondered what he talked about all night.

A few years later, my unstructured and largely undisciplined "one-way talks" with God received a little bit of direction when I learned about the "ACTS" way of praying. Christians love acronyms, don't they?

Adoration
Confession

Thanksgiving

Supplication

The ACTS prayer method helped open my eyes to the place of thanksgiving and worship in my prayer life. I'd already spent a good deal of time confessing my sins so that God wouldn't hate me, and then, once I'd gotten on his good side, dumped my list of requests. This helpful little acronym cleared up some oversights on my part. Prayer wasn't just about what I needed. Prayer became a practice where I saw what God had done and who God is. While that helped, I was still missing something very, very important.

QUIET, REPETITIOUS MONKS

I've used the ACTS prayer method and would encourage others to explore it, but I've been learning that prayer isn't limited to what I say to God. Prayer can also mean listening to God. In other words, my mouth needs to be shut and my mind tuned in to God.

That's probably what Jesus did on many of those long nights spent in prayer.

Listening prayer is both really simple and nearly impossible. We don't have to "do" anything in order to hear God. In fact, we can even listen for the voice of God while we walk, cook dinner, wash the dishes, mow the lawn, build something, drive a car, or do anything else that doesn't require constant concentration. Having said that, listening prayer also calls for emptying our minds of our own thoughts in order to focus on God, and *that* is really, really hard. It's especially hard today because our phones, computers, and tablets demand constant updates and interaction.

"Just snapped a picture of my awesome prayer retreat" is the kind of online update that misses the point.

Venturing into the woods or a wilderness area isn't a guarantee that our minds will be free from distractions. The men and women who first sought out solitude in the wilderness of Egypt in the fourth century found more than enough battles in their own minds. Without household projects, traffic jams, kids, jobs, and an array of technology, they found that prayer remained quite hard. They also discovered that once removed from

Henri Nouwen writes in *The Way of the Heart* about the nature of prayer:

> Thinking about God makes God into a subject that needs to be scrutinized or analyzed. Successful prayer is thus prayer that leads to new intellectual discoveries about God. Just as a psychologist studies a case and seeks to gain insight by trying to find coherence in all the available data, so someone who prays well should come to understand God better by thinking deeply about all that is known about him.

Nouwen adds:

> We find the best formulation of the prayer of the heart in the words of the Russian Theophan the Recluse: "To pray is to descend with the mind into the heart, and there to stand before the face of the Lord, ever-present, all-seeing, within you. . . ." There God's Spirit dwells and there the great encounter takes place.[2]

the temptations of the city, demons showed up to tempt them with far more regularity. Although moving into the desert helped simplify their lives, prayer remained a struggle for men and women who had left everything behind to make prayer a priority. Who doesn't have a hard time staying still in order to pray? Who isn't flooded with thoughts the moment you sit still?

The good news is that Christians have many different strategies for becoming quiet long enough to hear the voice of God. I resisted them for a while because I used to think that repetition was bad for prayer, let alone "recycling" what someone else wrote as a prayer. However, I've since learned that reciting simple prayers or slowly reading through a small passage of Scripture can break the distracting cycles of my mind and carve out a friendly spot for God to set up shop.

The one prayer that I turn to the most is the Jesus prayer: "Lord Jesus Christ, Son of God, have mercy on me, a sinner." It's a great way to begin prayer because let's face it: I usually have something to confess anyway.

PRAYING "THE DIVINE HOURS"

I often begin my day with this prayer:

> Lord God, almighty and everlasting Father, you have brought me in safety to this new day: Preserve me with your mighty power, that I may not fall into sin, nor be overcome by adversity; and in all I do direct me to the fulfilling of your purpose; through Jesus Christ my Lord. Amen.[3]

This confession from the Book of Common Prayer is a great way to end the day:

> Most merciful God, we confess that we have sinned against you in thought, word, and deed, by what we have done, and by what we have left undone. We have not loved you with our whole heart; we have not loved our neighbors as ourselves. We are truly sorry and we humbly repent. For the sake of your Son Jesus Christ, have mercy on us and forgive us; that we may delight in your will, and walk in your ways, to the glory of your Name. Amen.

This ancient prayer has been used by Christians as a tool to help train their minds to hear the voice of God. Some use it as a way to kick off a time of prayer, while others only use it if their minds start to wander, letting it renew their focus on the cross and the mercy of God to redeem us.

I've also used other memorized prayers at key moments in my day to help redirect my mind to God. While exercising I'll pray the Our Father and try to meditate on each part of the prayer. What evil am I asking God to deliver us from? Who do I need to forgive? How can I trust God to provide what we need for today?

The Divine Hours is a published series of daily prayers compiled by Phyllis Tickle using the Liturgy of the Hours and the Book of Common Prayer. Three volumes cover the different seasons of the year and a couple more lead up to special times of the year (Christmas and Easter). Each day has three readings and a final "compline" with Scripture readings and prayers from various points in church history. Some days I spend more time meditating on a passage of Scripture. Other days I freestyle my prayers.

The discipline of listening prayer has dramatically changed the way I approach prayer. My expectations have shifted dramatically, as I now expect God to speak. Some days I sense a leading or direction from God and other days I don't. Sometimes God drops in on me unannounced with a message. There are days when I'm left wondering if I really heard God speak or if it was my imagination.

Listening prayer and Christian survival are linked together. How else can we know when we are straying from God or need to adjust the course of our lives if we can't hear the voice of God? I'm well aware that this kind of prayer will be a challenge for many. When I started to practice listening prayer, I heard absolutely nothing. That promptly led to a crisis of faith. Is God real? Does God hate me? I jumped from one frantic conclusion to another.

Prayer is one Christian practice that relies on self-discipline and feedback from a trusted mentor or spiritual advisor. You need to ask hard questions about the times prayer "doesn't work" and the times you think you have heard from God but aren't sure. When I think God is leading me in a particular direction, I often check in with a trusted friend or relative to make sure I'm on the right track. Sometimes a "message from God" is downgraded to just a great idea. Other times the very thing I'm resisting is exactly what God has called me to do. The more an idea lingers and pesters me, the more likely God's speaking to me.

> "In honesty you have to admit to a wise man that prayer is not for the wise, not for the prudent, not for the sophisticated. Instead it is for those who recognize that in face of their deepest needs, all their wisdom is quite helpless. It is for those who are willing to persist in doing something that is both childish and crucial."
> —Frederick Buechner, *The Magnificent Defeat*[4]

Maybe you've always been open to the possibility that God could speak to you. Maybe this is brand new. And then perhaps you have a history of frustration and failure. Wherever you're coming from, there's a really good reason why I'm digging into the specifics of prayer. The church as we know it wouldn't exist without prayer.

PRAYER THAT SENDS US PACKING

If you've read the book of Acts and epistles of the New Testament, there's a good chance you know that Peter and Paul were both apostles with rather different callings. They were so different at times that they had sharp disagreements. Paul writes that he confronted Peter to set him straight. Although they clashed plenty of times, they shared something very important: a divine calling from God. We make a significant mistake if we think that such clarity of calling and belief is limited to apostles like them.

Peter never would have considered preaching the gospel to a Roman centurion and his household and relatives. Paul didn't know where to go on his missionary journey. He reached a dead end at Troas and only moved on to Macedonia when he had a vision of a man calling him to come help them. It doesn't strike me as fair that God would launch the church with a Holy Spirit bang and then leave future generations to sort things out for themselves with the Bible.

In fact, in one story after another, we find that many of the most dramatic conversions and ministries have come from spiritual encounters with God. In moments of prayer, meditation, visions, and dreams, God has directed saints to sell their possessions, serve the poor, negotiate peace among warring armies, and preach the gospel with boldness. In fact, you'll be hard pressed to find a significant movement in Christianity that wasn't sparked by prayer and the direct intervention of God empowering people to do extraordinary things.

We may be able to squeak by with a little bit of prayer here and there, but thriving as growing Christians has everything to do with our connection to Christ, our vine who makes us come to life and helps us bear fruit. If there is anything that could threaten your faith as a follower of Jesus, it's a lack of commitment to prayer. Without prayer we may do good things, but there's no telling whether we'll be directed by God, and we certainly won't have the benefit of God's power and resources.

DARK NIGHTS AND BREAKTHROUGH BREAKDOWNS

In my own Protestant tradition there isn't a whole lot written about the times we fail to find God or struggle with doubts. In fact, our focus on being saved or unsaved may even create a dynamic where we see faith as a switch that's either on or off, and if things aren't working, we fear that somehow we've lost our salvation or God isn't real after all. We don't have much of a grid for seasons of struggle, depression, and loneliness. Some have been told that God is either real and capable of showing up when we pray or God is fake and will not show up when we pray. But there's a third option. God can be both real and seemingly not present for a season.

I won't even begin to speculate about the potential causes for a dark night of the soul. However, I want you to know that you're in good company if you're going through one. In her personal letters, Mother Teresa wrote about living in a perpetual season where she didn't hear from God.

A SAINT LIVING IN DARKNESS

Mother Teresa set out to serve the poor after having several mystical encounters with Jesus in 1946. She wrote in those days about her encounters with "the Voice" who asked her to serve the poorest of the poor and about her passionate love for Jesus. However, once she began serving the poor in Calcutta, she entered a prolonged season of spiritual darkness and loneliness:

In a letter estimated to be from 1961, Teresa wrote: "Darkness is such that I really do not see—neither with my mind nor with my reason—the place of God in my soul is blank—There is no God in me—when the pain of longing is so great—I just long & long for God. . . . The torture and pain I can't explain."[5]

She persevered in faith as she served the poor even if she couldn't get a direct confirmation from God for long stretches of time.[6]

I have sensed the joy of the Lord when I do certain things. I'm well aware of God's guidance for specific things in my life. However, there are many days when I don't get a clear sense of God's direction. Some days are lonelier than others when I pray. I'm stuck with persevering by faith based on what God showed me.

Some traditions see this season of alienation and darkness as a bad thing. It certainly can be that. I don't think anyone should feel alienated from God for a long time. However, these situations are not without precedent. We're in good company if we have a season of darkness or emptiness. If we're always praying for spiritual breakthroughs and come up empty, we need to stop and ask what God is teaching us in this season of loneliness and silence. Sometimes a time of waiting and anticipation can be just the thing we need even if it's not what we want. Oftentimes the seasons of my greatest needs, doubts, and struggles have made me more reliant on God than any other and have strengthened my faith in ways that I never anticipated.

That isn't to say that we should crave a dark night of the soul or downplay how difficult one can be. Rather, we fail to see that God can even use these seasons for good. All is not lost if God seems distant.

Sometimes a dramatic story like Billy Graham's request that God would provide him with $23,000 discourages us from praying because we tell ourselves, I could never have faith like that!

However, Graham didn't start with prayers like that. He started his preaching career on lonely river banks, on street corners, and outside bars. Sometimes annoyed bartenders stepped outside to sock the young preacher in the face. Graham faced disappointments, struggles, and uncertainty over and over again. The more he stepped out in faith, the more he learned to rely on prayer.

If you're just trying to figure out how to survive as a Christian, I don't expect you to kneel down today and to ask God for a huge sum of money. Keep in mind, Graham was indecisive about whether to start the radio ministry. It took the prompting of some Christian friends to convince him to take a leap of faith.

That feels a lot like my own prayer life. I wrestle with uncertainty and fear until God somehow prompts me to make a specific request. Don't let prayer guilt prevent you from seeking God. Jesus wants us to make our thoughts known to God much like a child would speak to a parent. If we can get past our guilt and uncertainty, we will learn the exciting news that God can't wait to speak to us.

THE BIBLE

A SOURCE OF CRISIS AND HOPE

My wife has an old Leatherman camping knife that she always takes with us for our camping trips. You may find her hacking away at rope to make a tarp canopy over our tent, chopping apple wedges, or prying into place a stubborn leg on our camp stove with her knife. It's a handy little knife. In fact, it could be an essential survival tool if we ever lost our way on a hike and needed to build our own shelter for the night.

Put into the wrong hands (mine for instance), a knife could also prove detrimental to our safety—or at least my safety. I could just as well cut myself or carelessly leave the knife on the ground where someone could step on it. We generally keep the knife under my wife's capable supervision because we know that bloodletting will be minimized as long as she's in charge of it.

If you've ever had a run-in with an angry preacher shouting Scripture verses into a bullhorn, you've learned that the Bible can also be used as a weapon. Parents have kicked their own children out of their home, families have stopped speaking to each other, churches have divided, and plenty of friendships have ended because of disagreements over the Bible. I've spoken to friends and colleagues who have either left Christianity or struggled to stick with it because of what the Bible says. For all of the times that the Bible can bring comfort and direction, it can also disturb us and raise issues that unsettle our faith. It is both friend and foe at times—an essential tool for Christian survival that can easily be mishandled.

We'll address some specific topics in the following chapters, but as we sort out how to use the Bible as a source of hope for our survival as Christians, I want to ask a very basic, foundational question about the Bible. What exactly is the purpose of the Bible? The answer isn't quite so simple to figure out.

In my midtwenties I had my obligatory falling-out with the church. One of my main beefs with the church revolved around what I read in the Bible: I believed that our contemporary church meetings have very little in common with the small house church meetings described in Acts and the Epistles. Back then I believed that small and decentralized was "the way" to do church rather than one of many options. I used Scripture verses to justify my newfound doctrine that the early church moved from "house to house" and then used my blog to criticize the vast majority of churches in my circles. I lost a few friends along the way.

Perhaps you've also used the Bible like this: treating it like a reference guide to construct a "biblical" blueprint and then criticizing anyone who deviates from "God's plan." We can attach "biblical" to any number of concepts: biblical family, biblical manhood,[1] biblical womanhood,[2] biblical lifestyle, biblical family, biblical sex, biblical leadership, or biblical work. The assumption is that the Bible gives us definitive guidelines that are timeless and easy to apply to our lives. That's how I read the Bible when I went through my "know it all" phase with the church. I thought I'd found the only biblical way to "do" church. As my certainty increased, I became increasingly insufferable.

Ironically, the more I committed myself to the study of Scripture, the more my tidy categories fell apart. It wasn't that I couldn't find the truth in the Bible. Rather, I found so many truths and perspectives that I couldn't piece them together perfectly every time.

I'm by no means the most learned theologian, but I've devoted enough time to the study of Scripture that I've found the Bible more disruptive to my categories and blueprints than affirming. Isn't that what we should expect from a book that spans thousands of years and intersects with a variety of cultures and communities? In fact, I would go so far as saying that it is unbiblical to say that there is a "biblical" way to live.

IS THE BIBLE A BLUEPRINT OR A WORK OF ART?

Sometimes I've used the Bible as if it were a blueprint that spelled out the precise way to live as a Christian. I expected everyone to believe and practice just like me. I'm sure you've attended churches where you felt tremendous pressure to conform in all areas. I once met a pastor whose church was considering firing him because he didn't believe in the rapture. Other churches put pressure on families to conform to their specific biblical guidelines. I've had my own narrow theological guidelines that I've used to neatly divide my friends into insiders and outsiders.

Is the Bible supposed to do that? Does it give us specific guidelines to follow in any and every situation?

I have since found that the Bible functions more like a work of art.

We all know that paintings, poems, and stories have a range of meaning and can be interpreted in several ways within that range. As new generations view a painting or read a book, they can appreciate what it meant to the original author, what it meant to previous generations, and what it means to them in the present.

A painting can accurately portray an actual event. A poem can communicate a truth. Then again, there is a significant difference between a portrait that aims to capture a precise image of a person and an impressionist painting of a wheat field on a warm summer day where the wind gently courses through the heads of grain. In art and poetry, truths aren't always dropped on us in plain, bold letters. We have to talk about them with others and think about them, returning to them over time to ponder the meaning further.

Before you start piling the firewood to burn me at the stake, let's take a look at a few stories and then return to how we use the word *biblical*.

JUST GIVE ME THE RULES

A few years ago my wife and I attended a Columbus Blue Jackets game— that's an NHL hockey team. We sat in seats we'd picked up on the cheap from a local university since Julie was a graduate student, and I sat next to an adventurous Chinese family who had picked up the hockey tickets from the same campus box office. The man next to me didn't quite follow the game like me. I was jumping up at every shot on goal and then screaming and booing at the referees. He sat straight-faced with perfect posture. Who knows what he thought of me. Regardless, I decided it was my duty to educate this family on the basics of hockey. At the very least he needed to understand a few basic rules like offsides and icings.

Although the noise and our language barrier made it tough to communicate, I explained the basic rules of hockey. He nodded and asked a bunch of questions. He even stumped me with one of his observations. With this crash course in hockey, he at least understood why his neighbor went mental at certain points in the game. I even caught him clapping as the game progressed. Knowing a few rules is good enough for experiencing a hockey game, but knowing a few rules wouldn't help either of us all that

REVEALING THE SECRET IDENTITY OF MODERN PHARISEES

Modern pharisees look for ways to exclude those outside of their religious group who worship Jesus differently. They build walls between themselves and others.

They exclude people based on how they dress, who they know, where they hang out, what they listen to, how they worship, and how they practice their faith. Then again, who hasn't done something like that?

We all play the pharisee game, defining who is in and who is out, puffing up our own qualifications before God, insisting that we've got it more together than anyone else. The key to winning the pharisee game is to set up strict standards and to then exclude anyone who can't adhere to them. Describing God as merciful and gracious while also building walls between people and God's grace is virtually unbeatable in the pharisee game. That is, unless someone can prove that God is far more loving than expected.

much if we tried to actually play hockey. That requires both understanding the rules and the various ways to apply them to different situations. By the same token, just learning the rules is a lousy way to live as a Christian. In fact, when Jesus criticized the Pharisees, he compared them to children playing games in the marketplace where they imitated weddings and funerals by following the rules and protocols but never really perceived what was going on. They were playing at religion, using the Scriptures to develop games with strict rules that set them apart as insiders.

No one wants to reduce the Bible to rules, but if we start talking about the alternatives, we may become uncomfortable. If the Bible isn't about learning the rules and following them to the letter, aren't we abandoning the truth of the Bible? Are we failing to hold on to the message from God?

Unless you're a pastor or a student with a degree in Bible, you probably don't know too much about the way the battle between liberal and conservative theology has impacted the way we read the Bible. In fact, you probably don't care. It's important, but I don't want to lose you, so I'll be painfully brief. Many liberal theologians in the 1800s and 1900s started teaching that the Bible was never intended to relate true, historical stories to us. Rather, it was mainly intended to give us a spiritual experience with God that could be life transforming, but not because you were following specific rules from the Bible. In response to that, conservative theologians claimed that the Bible was 100 percent historically accurate since it was inspired by the Holy Spirit and that the true followers of Jesus applied the teachings of the Bible literally to their lives. Here's an extremely generalized summary:

> Conservative = Read the Bible literally and historically in order to obey it.
> Liberal = Read the Bible for spiritual insights.

Got it?

Here's where we have our problem. Conservatives are absolutely correct about the historical reliability of the Bible, even if they sometimes get stuck on language issues, such as the length of a "day" in Genesis 1.[3] On the other hand, the liberals were onto something about the spiritual purpose of the Bible. If there is one purpose for the Bible, it isn't to prove that the Bible is true; it's to help us meet God. At least, that's what Jesus said.

In criticizing the Jewish leaders, Jesus said, "You study the Scriptures diligently because you think that in them you have eternal life. These are the very Scriptures that testify about me" (John 5:39). For all of my hard work learning the Bible over the years, the one thing that matters most is meeting the risen Christ. Some theologians speak of the Bible as a sign that points us to God. The sign must be accurate and it is extremely important, but if we just spent our days learning more and more about the sign, we'll never go to the place the sign is telling us about. Treating a sign as the destination misses the point of the sign. My family used to travel to New York City for shows, but we never stopped at the signs outside of New York to sit and wait for the show to begin. The sign isn't where the action happens.

This can be uncomfortable for many of us. Are we opening the door for false doctrine? That's always a possibility no matter how much you try to value the Bible. The point is that we shouldn't feel pressure to prove how much we value the Bible if we understand that the goal of the Bible is to help us encounter God. The historicity of the Bible matters because the kinds of encounters we read about can be true for us, but we read about them so we can experience them too, not just to know about them or to prove them. While we may not stumble into burning bushes, there is every reason to believe that God can heal our personal wounds, win spiritual victories, and guide his people into truth through the Holy Spirit.

When God promised the Israelites that the law would be written in their hearts, we have a clue about the future of the Bible. One day the rules

"Believing in him is not the same as believing things about him such as that he was born of a virgin and raised Lazarus from the dead. Instead, it is a matter of giving our hearts to him, of come hell or high water putting our money on him, the way a child believes in a mother or a father, the way a mother or a father believes in a child."
—Frederick Buechner, *Secrets in the Dark*[4]

wouldn't matter so much as loving God and obeying out of a commitment to God rather than a desire to follow the rules perfectly.

HOW MISUSING THE BIBLE CAUSES PROBLEMS

Even if we start reading the Bible with the best of intentions, we can end up being limited by our past experiences and assumptions. I spoke to one young woman who was serving the poor in the inner city who couldn't read the Bible—at least not at that point in her life. While completely committed to following Jesus, the leaders in her childhood church had used the Bible as a weapon to condemn and control others. The Bible didn't mean good news, liberation, and freedom. In fact, it became the exact opposite message. With the wrong motivations and the wrong interpretation, the Bible can imprison and wound. That woman still wanted to read the Bible again someday, but she just didn't see a way out of her past yet.

How could a book of good news become bad news? How could someone have such a terrible experience with the Bible?

In my own life, I've seen this happen when I become too attached to a particular reading of the Bible and then hinged my entire faith on that particular interpretation. For example, this is how we end up with Christians fighting over the interpretation of Genesis 1–2 with so much passion. I used to think that the integrity of the Bible hinged on proving the earth was created in six literal days. If I couldn't prove a young earth, then the Bible wasn't true, and if the Bible wasn't true, then everything I believed about God would collapse. You could say that my thinking has evolved since then.

While there are many plausible explanations for resolving an old earth with Genesis 1–2, the point is that our faith doesn't hinge on perfect answers. Our faith doesn't hinge on the details of a story about the Creator. Our faith hinges on whether that Creator is still redeeming and re-creating people today. Genesis 1–2 points us to the creator God who has conquered sin today. The truthfulness of Genesis 1–2 matters, however it happened, but we haven't won anything if we can "prove" that Genesis 1–2 took place in six literal days. We win when we receive the new creation of Christ. Protecting the Bible alone leads to all kinds of conflict and destruction that prevents us from experiencing God's new creation in our lives.

AN EVOLVING DEBATE

Evolution has been a particularly contentious issue for many Christians in America where they have felt forced to choose between the scientific explanation for the creation of our world and the Bible's. Can the two be reconciled?

For years, I didn't think they could. In my senior year of high school I wrote a report challenging the evidence for evolution. I didn't realize that when Darwin's work first arrived on the scene, many Christians saw no conflict with Christianity and evolution.

Noted American botanist Asa Gray collaborated with Darwin and widely supported his work while serving as a deacon at his church. Gray wrote in favor of theistic evolution and found support among legendary conservative theologians A. A. Hodge and B. B. Warfield.

That isn't to say Christians weren't opposed to evolution. Charles Hodge and William Jennings Bryan famously spoke out against the possibility of evolution erasing the need for God. However, the voice of Christianity when it comes to interpreting Genesis 1–2 has hardly been unanimous from the early days of Darwin's work.

I've spoken to plenty of Christians who have experienced the sharp edge of the Bible in the hands of someone who used it as a weapon for control, personal justification, or as a way of protecting their faith. No one wants to be wrong about the Bible, and out of the fear of being wrong, we can make the mistake of attacking anyone who disagrees.

Whether offering simple answers or attacking anyone who disagrees with my perspective, I've learned that the times I'm most combative are often when I'm least secure about what I believe.

STOP TRYING TO BE "BIBLICAL"

I'm suggesting a subtle shift in perspective regarding the Bible. At bare minimum, I'm saying that we should not seek to be "biblical." Being biblical isn't even a concept in the Bible. If you want to develop a "biblical" approach to marriage, you need to resolve teachings in cultures that included concubines, multiple wives, women viewed as property, and sex cults. If you want to develop a "biblical" approach to conflict management, you need to resolve Solomon's "trigger happy" use of Benaiah to kill his opponents and Jesus' commands to turn the other cheek and to forgive without limit. If you want to talk about "biblical" leadership, you have to take into account patriarchy, monarchy, the role of prophets, the Jewish conception of rabbis, the education of women in the ancient world, and the Greek conception of female oracles. Living "biblically" is rarely plain and simple. Even during *The Year of Living Biblically*, A. J. Jacobs struggled to adapt the Bible's teachings on owning slaves—that is, until an aspiring young writer volunteered for the "position" during his year-long experiment of following the Bible as literally as possible.

The question for us today isn't "Am I doing the Bible right?" The question is this: "Am I living like Jesus?"

We can try to be biblical and end up being *unlike* Jesus. Just following the Bible will not teach us to love, forgive, or redeem. Using the Bible to guide us to Jesus will always make us "biblical," but we won't necessarily be able to resolve everything in our lives perfectly with the Bible. Perhaps a simple example would help here.

I've often heard the teaching "Don't let the sun go down on your anger" applied very literally: immediately resolve any conflict (see Eph. 4:26). But being angry isn't necessarily sinful, though it's so easy to sin when you're angry. Like when he confronted Cain (Gen. 4:6), God in this command is warning us: don't put off dealing with your anger. The problem with anger is that sometimes we need time to step out of a situation to understand it fully. I have found that in certain situations I need to sleep on something before I can figure out what's really going on. If I'm annoyed at my wife about something she said, it's often good for me to sit on it and to gain a clear picture of what's really bugging me. Often the event that made me angry just touched on a bigger issue that we need to talk about. Sometimes by actually "letting the sun go down on my anger," I'm able to be less reactive and angry and we end up resolving conflict with less drama.

I can think of plenty of ways my approach is "biblical," even if it's not precisely following the Bible to the exact letter. Paul wrote that love is patient and love is kind. Waiting to resolve a conflict until I understand a

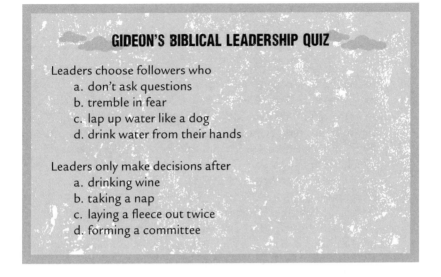

GIDEON'S BIBLICAL LEADERSHIP QUIZ

Leaders choose followers who
  a. don't ask questions
  b. tremble in fear
  c. lap up water like a dog
  d. drink water from their hands

Leaders only make decisions after
  a. drinking wine
  b. taking a nap
  c. laying a fleece out twice
  d. forming a committee

situation better can be both patient and kind. Believe me, there are plenty of times when I don't like waiting to resolve conflict. This isn't the easy way in the short run, but I've seen it play out far better in the long term.

It's quite possible to use the Bible in very unbiblical ways. I could demand that we resolve a disagreement before either of us is ready to talk about it because the Bible demands that we deal with our anger immediately. This is the kind of stuff that Jesus called straining a gnat and swallowing a camel. I could be so concerned with following the precise "rules" of Scripture that in doing so I could fail to love my wife as Christ loved the church. This is the resounding theme in the Prophets. God's people had obsessed over the rules for sacrifices and festivals to the point that they had completely lost touch with actually worshipping God.

What is the alternate to this rule-following, camel-swallowing obsession? What if we thought of reading the Bible as simply having a good time with God?

A NEW KIND OF HAPPY HOUR

When I read about the writers of the Psalms delighting in the law of the Lord, there were times when I've wondered whether we were reading the same stuff. Did that guy even read Leviticus? Care to casually flip through

GOING BROKE ONCE EVERY FIFTY YEARS

One of the least delightful chapters in the Bible for Americans today has to be Leviticus 25. First of all, yes, Leviticus is a real book in the Bible. Secondly, it's not just about priests. Leviticus deals with laws that governed God's people, especially the redistribution of property every fifty years.

Did you work hard to expand your property for the past forty-nine years? Too bad. The Year of Jubilee demands that everyone returns to their ancestral land. Slaves go free. Debts are forgiven.

Americans lose their minds trying to apply this passage.

The first time I read about the Year of Jubilee, I had just bought a house, and I was trying to figure out what it would feel like to hand over our property to someone else. It wasn't a great feeling. However, the Year of Jubilee also exposed the dangers of my attachment to the things that belong to God alone. It wasn't a delightful lesson, but it's one I return to often.

Numbers? I don't really need to sit up all night pondering how many shekels it would cost me if my neighbor's ox stumbled into a hole in my yard. I also find the parts about marrying a woman from a conquered tribe or buying a few slaves to be a little outdated. I'm progressive like that.

How does one delight in the Bible?

I have found that the more I read the Bible, the more I delight in it. That's a hard sell. Indeed at first, reading the Bible will mostly feel like hard work. Sometimes "epiphanies" will be few and far between. However, if you keep with it, there's usually a reward.

At this point in my life, I am an avid gardener, but it has not always been so. My wife had to convince me to dig up a plot of dirt when we were first married, and I did very little of the digging for the fence or the planting. She was completely on her own for it, and the amount of weeding required in our new plot was more than one person could handle.

A few years later, we started a garden in our new home, and we grew a little patch of lettuce and a few tomato plants. I had a lot more fun with this garden, and everything tasted so much better when we grew it ourselves.

I started to crave more tomatoes and lettuce. I even began to think about what else we could grow. How about spinach, carrots, radishes, or green beans? In the years that followed our garden space grew, and we added more plants. I now crave fresh carrots from our garden and ripe tomatoes with slices of mozzarella cheese and basil—basil that we also grow in our garden.

Getting to that point took a lot of hard work. We tilled one garden plot from scratch. The next we weeded constantly in a community plot. Another I built with raised beds. Each time I knew that my hard work in the garden would bring tremendous rewards. From fresh lettuce and Swiss chard to green beans and garlic, we had a much easier time making sacrifices for the sake of our garden after enjoying its harvest for a few years.

We read in Psalm 119:54-56, "Your decrees are the theme of my song wherever I lodge. In the night, LORD, I remember your name, that I may keep your law. This has been my practice: I obey your precepts."

This isn't something you learn at a weekend seminar or pick up in a book. It's a learned discipline that takes shape over time. It's a practice—which means you'll probably do it badly for a season until you get the hang of it and see the ways your life changes. Each person's practices may look a little different. Results may even look different as well. However, the goal for all remains the same: learning to delight in God by interacting with Scripture.

As we talk about survival, we'll look at a range of Christian beliefs rather than advancing the agenda of one particular group. Sometimes the way I read the Bible doesn't make sense to someone else.

We can't shy away from the hard questions that could wreck the faith of some. In fact, we have a lot more to worry about if we can't face the challenging questions of the Bible. Our next chapter will address the most disturbing passages in Scripture related to God. These passages have both damaged the faith of some and prevented others from even considering Christianity. Survival as followers of Jesus doesn't depend on finding the perfect answer, but many have found these passages troubling enough to reconsider their beliefs.

VIOLENT BIBLE STORIES

DELIVER US FROM GOD?

MARCION OF SINOPE GREW up in the church during the early second century A.D. and enjoyed many advantages in education and work. His father was a bishop so he knew Scripture very well, most likely benefited from a classical education, and ran a successful shipping business. Marcion even made significant donations to the church. If you looked at his profile—wealthy and educated—you could say he was the ideal church member.

Everything changed for Marcion when he allegedly seduced a virgin, and his father excommunicated him. Whatever the reason for his father expelling him, Marcion quickly reestablished himself in Rome around A.D. 140, some 1,500 miles (2,400 km) west, where he refashioned himself as a religious leader and continued to support the church. However, after a few years, Marcion began to reshape his theology along the lines of dualistic thinkers who separated matter as evil and spirit as good. In particular, he found the Old Testament problematic—not an uncommon development in that day.

As Marcion expanded his band of followers, he put together a canon of Scripture that relied principally on Paul's epistles, Luke's gospel, and Acts. This was a list of books he accepted as Holy Scripture. Marcion taught that the "violent" God of the Old Testament had nothing in common with the God revealed in Jesus. In fact, Jesus revealed a completely different

God. Whereas Jesus taught love of enemies, Marcion pointed out that the God of the Old Testament used war and vengeance to get his way.

The church in Rome declared Marcion a heretic for this teaching and for many of his other doctrines. However, his movement lasted four hundred years because of Marcion's deft organizing, deep pockets, and appeal to Christians in a culture influenced by Greek philosophical thinking that found Judaism repellent (even the Jews were divided between traditionalists who rejected Greek culture and the Hellenists who embraced it). Marcion found a ready audience among people who struggled to connect the Old and New Testaments. Many of their problems with the Bible could be solved by taking scissors, or the ancient equivalent, to their Scripture scrolls.

Marcion was among the first to make a public break between the Old Testament and the New Testament, and many since have continued to struggle with the same issues he confronted. A variety of heresies such as Gnosticism and Manichaeism have quite a bit in common with Marcion's religious philosophy. While Marcion's issues with the Old Testament were many, perhaps the hardest points to reconcile with the New Testament have to do with the violence of God. How can God command the eradication of

Christians aren't the only ones who struggle with the God they find in the Bible. Former Orthodox Jew Shalom Auslander wrote in his memoir,

> When I was a child, my parents and teachers told me about a man who was very strong. They told me he could destroy the whole world. They told me he could lift mountains. They told me he could part the sea. It was important to keep the man happy. When we obeyed what the man had commanded, the man liked us. He liked us so much that he killed anyone who didn't like us. But when we didn't obey what he commanded, he didn't like us. He hated us. Some days he hated us so much, he killed us; other days he let other people kill us. We call these days "holidays."[1]

entire towns and nations in one part of the Bible and then command us to love our enemies in the next part?

I have spoken to several former Christians recently who can't reconcile themselves to these Bible stories. They view the God of the Old Testament as petty, vengeful, and bloodthirsty, while Jesus stands for peace and tolerance. Some leave the faith over this, others ponder it quietly, still others suggest that the Jews in the Old Testament didn't actually hear God, and some others end up imitating Marcion, cutting off the Old Testament from Jesus and the New Testament.

Our challenges are many. On the one hand we don't want to take scissors to the Bible merely to match it with our sensibilities. If God is truly God, then we are in no position to stand in judgment. However, there is a space for honest followers of Jesus to humbly ask, "How can we reconcile these two very different pictures of God in our inspired Scriptures?"

I'll be the first to admit that my own thinking here is a work in progress. There is a spectrum of beliefs on this subject. My goal isn't to provide "the" answer. Rather, I hope to introduce some of the complex issues at play here and to provide some lines of thinking that may help you continue thinking about this difficult topic.

The Bible depicts its fair share of violence and injustice. In fact, many biblical passages describe God's presence in the midst of violent conflicts, even ones he purportedly caused. God's presence in the following events stands out:

The Flood
The Destruction of Sodom and Gomorrah
The Conquest of Canaan
The Fall of Samaria to Assyria
The Fall of Jerusalem to Babylon

In each of these stories, the Old Testament authors portray God as either directly or indirectly sending destruction on different people groups. These stories coexist alongside gracious covenants with Noah, Abraham, Jacob, Moses, and David.

I especially want to avoid trite answers such as, "God killed the Canaanites because he is holy." I can understand that there is a line of reasoning behind a statement like that, but it overlooks a pretty big problem: isn't genocide sinful in the first place?

That isn't the only problem we'll have to consider as we try to reconcile the love of God with the stories in the Old Testament about God's violent commands and actions.

HOW TO DESCRIBE A "VIOLENT" GOD

One of the most helpful starting places in a discussion like this is a complete picture of how the writers of the Old Testament described their God YHWH (this is an abbreviation of the full name "Yahweh")—a name translated "LORD" with small capital letters in most English Bibles. There's no question that the Old Testament writers talked about fearing God and the anger of God. They attributed the tragedy of the exile to God's judgment for their unfaithfulness. Of particular concern here is the conquest of Canaan in which God seemingly sanctions genocide. While we have many stories that may make us feel uneasy around such a God, the writers of the Old Testament clearly see some things that we dare not overlook.

In his book *God Behaving Badly: Is the God of the Old Testament Angry, Sexist, and Racist?*, professor David Lamb suggests that we start with the complete picture the writers of Scripture painted of YHWH.[2] They regularly described YHWH as patient and full of loving-kindness. In fact, they believed that things could have been "worse" if YHWH wasn't so kind and patient.

This line of thinking began with the exodus and ran right through the Psalms and the Prophets to the return from exile. We see this declaration about God after the exodus from Egypt: "He passed in front of Moses, proclaiming, 'The LORD, the LORD, the compassionate and gracious God, slow to anger, abounding in love and faithfulness'" (Exod. 34:6). Once YHWH made this declaration, it became one of the most common descriptors for YHWH by the Israelites, even when they passed through some of the most trying moments in their history. Given plenty of opportunities to question this title for their God, it shows up over and over again in both the poems and prophetic oracles of Israel.

The Psalms start to look like the poets were either plagiarizing each other or one of them had an intense case of writer's block and settled on repetition. Then again, they could have really wanted to make an important point about YHWH. "But you, LORD, are a compassionate and gracious God, slow to anger, abounding in love and faithfulness" (Ps. 86:15). Another psalm shortens it a bit: "The LORD is compassionate and gracious, slow to anger, abounding in love" (Ps. 103:8). We may as well say ditto for Psalm 145:8.

Jonah thought that God was actually too merciful. After God spared Nineveh, Jonah complained to God, "Isn't this what I said, LORD, when I was still at home? That is what I tried to forestall by fleeing to Tarshish. I knew that you are a gracious and compassionate God, slow to anger and abounding in love, a God who relents from sending calamity" (Jonah 4:2). In other words, while some of us only imagine a violent and vengeful God staring down at us with arching angry eyebrows and a lightning bolt in his right hand, Jonah saw a spiritual softie, eager to forgive and to spare the guilty from punishment.

Even the lesser-known prophets say the same thing about God. Not that many Christians today could even find Nahum in their Bibles if challenged to a "sword drill," but all the same, he picks up on the same theme: "The LORD is slow to anger but great in power; the LORD will not leave the guilty unpunished. His way is in the whirlwind and the storm, and clouds are the dust of his feet" (Nah. 1:3). After the calamity of the exile and the uncertainty of the return to Israel, the prophet Joel offered some practical advice: "Rend your heart and not your garments. Return to the LORD your God, for he is gracious and compassionate, slow to anger and abounding in love, and he relents from sending calamity" (Joel 2:13). Note also how Joel implies that the people abandoned YHWH. He sees the exile as a problem where the people abandoned God, not vice versa.

The consistent theme throughout the Old Testament is that YHWH is gracious, kind, and compassionate, but YHWH also won't tolerate people who merely go through the motions, exploit others, or pursue their own course forever. YHWH is patient and even more patient than we can imagine or could deserve, but that patience has a limit. And even if you've tried the patience of YHWH, there is always a chance to repent and to be restored. Judgment may come, but it's never the last word. Nehemiah sums this up well: "They refused to listen and failed to remember the miracles you performed among them. They became stiff-necked and in their rebellion appointed a leader in order to return to their slavery. But you are a forgiving God, gracious and compassionate, slow to anger and abounding in love. Therefore you did not desert them" (Neh. 9:17). Once again, calamity struck because the people abandoned YHWH.

In addition, YHWH was quite unlike other so-called gods worshipped in the ancient world; these would-be deities were violent, petty, and dehumanizing. At the heart of the conflict in many Old Testament stories is the unfaithfulness of the Israelites as they worshipped foreign gods that demanded the sacrifice of children and integrated prostitution into their worship. YHWH's requirements surrounding the sacrifices of livestock rather than exploiting women or killing children suddenly paints the God of the Israelites in a strikingly positive light. We could say that the God of the Jews was by far the most merciful and liberating god in the ancient world.

In fact, part of the challenge with idolatry may have been that the worship of YHWH was so counterintuitive: many Jews didn't think it would work. They wanted to cover their bases by worshipping more "traditional" gods. As the Israelites wavered from one god to another and eventually found their way back to YHWH from time to time, YHWH patiently waited like a jilted lover (see Hos. 2:14–23). Over and over again, YHWH offered promises to the Israelites: If you obey my commands and serve me alone, things will go well for you. Over and over again, the Israelites turned away. We can rightly ask what we expect of God when the Israelites called on false gods for deliverance when a foreign superpower invaded their land.

Unlike so many other peoples who were integrated into the Babylonian Empire, the Jewish people were allowed not only to survive but also to maintain their own identity in exile. In an unprecedented move, they were even able to return to their land by royal decree. All of this was attributed to the love and patience of YHWH.

While we'll have plenty to say in the following section about the violence of God, the Bible doesn't present us with a simple picture. Whatever we know about the violence of God must also be reconciled with the many verses about the ways God patiently loved and blessed his people, even when they were not deserving of such treatment.

WHY WORSHIP FALSE GODS?

The casual reader of the books of Samuel and Kings may grow frustrated with the Israelites. Why can't these people get their act together and worship YHWH, the true God? Why bother with all of these false gods made of wood and stone? As crazy as their version of idolatry sounds to us, their reasoning may not be quite so crazy once we take a little closer look. People today want many of the same things. They just rely on different means like money or political power to attain them. Here are some factors the Israelites would have considered when worshipping idols:

Sex: Many false gods incorporated temple prostitution into their worship. And if that wasn't incentive enough, the Israelites also married foreign women who wanted to keep their false gods around. Hello Solomon.

Rain: The land of Israel lacked reliable irrigation options, unlike Egypt and Babylon where rivers provided all of the water farmers required. Avoiding a famine meant regular rains became essential. Worshipping false gods became a "dry season" insurance policy.

Protection: Whether seeking to win over a foreign power as an ally or as a desperate gamble during an invasion, the Israelites weren't above seeking backup plans in case YHWH let them down.

False Prophets: The Israelites also relied on false gods because false prophets trumpeted the greatness of these deities, deceiving the people.

HOW TO SURVIVE IN TRIBAL CULTURE

One of the most difficult Old Testament stories to reconcile with the teachings of Jesus is the conquest of Canaan. The book of Joshua doesn't dress up the details. God sent the Israelites into Canaan with the goal of wiping out the people living there, lest they end up worshipping their false gods. This is all viewed as a fulfillment of God's promise to Abraham that his descendants would one day inherit the land of Canaan once the sins of the Canaanites reached their full measure.

This detail about the sins of the Canaanites is an interesting part of the background in this story. Should we presume that a full-scale repentance like what Jonah witnessed in Nineveh would have prompted God to spare the Canaanites and to figure out a way for them to coexist with the Israelites? In fact, if they had given up on false gods, then the key flashpoint between them and Israel would have been removed.

The nature of the invasion of Canaan was very much tied to judgment for the evil they had done. This was a very specific situation involving the historic actions of several tribes and cities. At no point in this story do we find a precedent for God approving a similar course of action in the future. Just as the flood was a one-time judgment, so too was the invasion of Canaan. The Israelites benefited from this judgment and were used in this particular instance as an instrument of God, but that does not mean the Israelites forever became the hammer of God for judging nations.

What did the Canaanites do that was so bad? We can start with what we do know: they regularly sacrificed children to their deities. In addition, they attacked the Israelites while they were wandering in the wilderness. While we may not think this makes them worthy of being wiped out completely, it is clear that the Canaanites were hardly innocent bystanders. Their actions would prompt an international crisis if the same happened in today's world.

Provided we can start by describing the invasion of Canaan as a unique situation where God used the Israelites to judge the specific sins of specific people, we can look at another tension in the narrative throughout Exodus, Deuteronomy, and Joshua. The Israelites were a people without a home in a hostile setting. The Egyptians had tried to chase them down in the wilderness, the nations east of the Jordan River attacked them when they tried to pass through, and the Canaanites were understandably ready to fight. What options did the Israelites have?

They could return to Egypt.

They could continue to wander in the wilderness.

They could try to settle east of the Jordan and pack themselves into smaller settlements.

They could invade Canaan.

Aside from being used by God to judge the Canaanites, the Israelites were also in an extremely difficult situation. It's one thing to escape slavery, but it's quite another matter to settle an entire nation of people in a new country—a historical anomaly, in fact (see 2 Sam. 7:23). All of the viable farmland was settled. That isn't to say that all bets are off, and they could kill whomever they liked. Rather, this story is about a band of former slaves who didn't have any attractive options. This wasn't a matter of a powerful nation exploiting a lesser people. The conquest of Canaan pitted an extreme underdog against highly organized armies with fortifications. We usually think of genocide as a powerful nation killing off a weaker minority. Just about every instance of genocide pits a powerful majority or a heavily militarized minority against a vulnerable minority.

In the case of Canaan, the weak people of Israel with every disadvantage attacked powerful cities that enjoyed every advantage over them. The Israelites had nowhere to go and nothing to lose. The Canaanites had the weight of God's judgment hanging over them and were in the wrong place at the wrong time.

There's no escaping the brutality of the conquest of Canaan. Completely wiping out a city under any other circumstances would be considered a war crime today. I don't think we can reach a place where we'll ever be fully comfortable with the events described in Joshua, but we can at least gather some perspective about the various forces at play in the situation. Does it make a difference that God sided with a band of homeless former slaves? Troubling as some parts of this story remain, we can see more connections with the rest of the Old Testament and the teachings of the New Testament. YHWH takes the side of the poor and oppressed, but in this one situation, the ramifications are difficult to untangle.

IS GOD CONSISTENTLY VIOLENT?

David is a complex character in the Bible whom we'll look at a few times throughout this guide to survive. For now, let's consider what happened when David aspired to build God's temple. Before David could start construction, God stopped him because he was a man of war. God did not want a warrior to build his house of worship.

We may rightly wonder, "Wait a second, wasn't David doing God's work?

Wasn't killing Philistines *the thing* back then?" This encounter with God suggests that David's violent past wasn't exactly ideal. While God certainly gave Israel victories in battle, God also didn't want his temple to have the stain of blood on it.

We could look at this in a few different ways. On the one hand, we could say that YHWH is inconsistent. Did God want David to fight those battles or not? On the other hand, we could say that perhaps God is able to handle tension much better than we are. While the consistent desire of YHWH throughout the Prophets is to beat swords into ploughshares, he's still willing to meet his people where they're at—even if it's in combat. And if YHWH could meet David in battle, he at least drew a line in the sand: Now that you have peace in your land, I will build my house of prayer under the leadership of a man of peace.

It's not perfect, but then God is dealing with people who make sinful choices. The raw materials are not exactly top notch at the start. However, there's a progression moving God's people away from violence. In fact, we could say that God moved his people from tribal warriors to a powerful nation who built temples and welcomed foreigners.

The future that God always imagines in the Old Testament is one with peace and justice where everyone can enjoy their own vineyards and crops. God does not present a future where his people will roam the earth as a marauding army. Their swords will become second-rate farm tools before they're ever raised in anger again.

CAN WE FIND RESOLUTION FOR A VIOLENT GOD?

I spoke some time ago to a friend who became an atheist because she couldn't accept the ways Christians judged and condemned others, especially her LGBT friends. With the way some Christians spoke about the fiery fate of LGBT individuals, she didn't see any way to resolve her friends with her faith. I didn't have a secret revelation from the Bible that could resolve the matter for her in five minutes, but I did have a couple of ideas about some potential ways to read the Bible's passages about homosexuality. As I shared a few possible interpretations of these passages, I could sense the tension between us lessen. Her defenses fell, and she said, "Oh, I'd never thought of those possibilities before."

I hope I can give you the same kind of hope as you wrestle with the violence of God. There just may be some possibilities you haven't considered before and they'll help you wrestle with some of the most difficult passages of the Bible.

However we explain the Old Testament story about Joshua and the conquest of Canaan, there's no escaping its place in the Bible. Joshua states that a lot of people died. It should disturb us. That God would be involved in this should unsettle us—especially in light of God's future plans for peace and the message of Jesus to love enemies.

It's striking that the Jewish people and the early church both held on to the book of Joshua along with the oracles of the prophets that spoke of a peaceful future. Who would blame them for tossing Joshua because it didn't fit with a more palatable book like Isaiah? To their credit, they kept the records passed down to them. The tough parts belong in the

DID JESUS CONDONE VIOLENCE?

Jesus said a Roman centurion
   a. had to quit the army
   b. was an enemy of God and the Jews
   c. had the most faith in all of Israel
   d. needed to train the Jews for a rebellion

Jesus told his followers to carry
   a. fishing nets
   b. extra money
   c. swords
   d. tiny Torah scroll tracts to unroll and give out in each
      city

Jesus rebuked Peter for
   a. calling down fire from heaven
   b. cheating through the Holy Spirit when asked if Jesus
      was the Messiah
   c. cutting off a man's ear
   d. his poor aim when cutting off a man's ear

story too. And if we consider that the Bible is inspired by the Spirit of God, we should ask what the Holy Spirit is telling us by including such diverse stories related to God and violence.

I don't expect a short chapter to resolve a big issue like this for most readers in one sitting. You may have questions I haven't addressed. You may not like my answers. You may need more time to process it all. I know I do.

However, I hope you can at least see the tension here. If there isn't a cut-and-dry way to explain the violence of God in Joshua, there also aren't grounds for dismissing God without further consideration. The situation is far more complex than we would expect in either direction. In fact, if the Bible could provide a pat answer explaining the violence of God, we may actually end up being even more suspicious. Rather, we have been presented with passages where God commands warriors into battle and other passages where God predicts a future without war. Maybe our dislike for the book of Joshua means we're exactly on the same page with God—that we've captured the message of Jesus.

Is it possible that the Bible gives us just enough to confuse us while also pointing to the kind of future we long for? However we resolve God's actions in the past, we can all agree that we desire the same kind of future as God: one with peace, freedom from fear, and lots and lots of vineyards.

One of the most pressing questions I face when I encounter this passage is whether I'm holding God to higher standards than I'm holding myself. I've voted for politicians who have then invaded other countries. And while I've had some misgivings about some of these wars, I can't say that I'm a 100 percent pacifist. As much as I want to completely disavow violence, especially at a state level, I can't quite see how letting someone kill my friends and family does justice to the image of God. In that respect, I have to accept that if I'm willing to see situations where violence may be permissible, I have to remain open to the same possibility for God.

Perhaps the involvement of God in any kind of violent conquest is too much for those who are committed to pacifism. I can appreciate that.

Whatever more there is to say, if this chapter has left you conflicted and dissatisfied, then you're probably in a good place. That's most likely the very thing we're supposed to take away from these stories.

DELIVER US FROM EVIL

IS GOD LATE?

WHEN WE TALK ABOUT renowned missionary Hudson Taylor, we tend to focus on his faith in Christ, commitment to adopting the Chinese culture when he preached, medical work among the poor, and his complete dependence on God for his financial provision. However, the private life of Hudson Taylor was no picnic, and his is an instructive life to consider when we discuss the place of God in matters of pain and suffering.

For starters, Taylor lost seven children at a very young age, including stillborn twins to his second wife, Jennie, while traveling on a ship to China. That's right, his first wife Maria passed away while they were ministering in China. Although Taylor saw almost as many children survive into adulthood, bearing him many grandchildren, the extent of his suffering didn't end with the loss of a beloved wife and children. Taylor was robbed and his medical supplies were torched during his first trip to China. The other missionaries didn't care for his mission society practice of dressing like the Chinese, and the British government really didn't like how he visited politically sensitive regions, leading to a series of smear campaigns against his missionary work. Taylor's mission building was burned and many of the missionaries on his team were beaten during a riot. Taylor was also nearly paralyzed when he fell off a riverboat. Am I pushing the believability of this too far if I add that he was nearly shipwrecked several times in typhoons?

59

There's no doubt that Taylor was doing the work of God. His contemporaries were so bold as to compare his significance to the apostle Paul. Between England and China, Taylor served thousands upon thousands as a doctor and preacher. There are few ministers who have so effectively embodied the holistic commitment of Christ to healing both body and soul. If anything, we would expect this man and his family to have enjoyed special protection from God. Why would God permit this man who so boldly served others to suffer so much?

I have seen similar circumstances play out among certain friends of mine in ministry. One woman has worked tirelessly with a renowned Christian charity, but her family disapproves of her work. In fact, they actively discourage her, using the Bible to tear her down. Another family I know is involved in leading multiple church plants, but they had to take time off after they lost a young child. I could go on with stories of good, righteous people doing God's work who have suffered much.

What gives? Isn't God supposed to be a fortress, shield, and strong tower, the One who protects the righteous?

Our questions may persist in the face of national tragedy or natural disasters. For every story of someone who miraculously survives and credits God or "angels," there are hundreds of thousands of others who don't make it when earthquakes, tsunamis, hurricanes, or tornadoes strike. Did God or the angels fail? Why are some spared and others afflicted?

Questions like these are always lingering in the back of my mind whether or not I'm suffering, and I know I'm not alone. A recent LifeWay poll[1] found that the majority of Americans were either confused or disturbed by God when trying to sort out the place of God in the midst of a tragedy. While 33 percent said they "trust God more" in the midst of a disaster, the rest shared the following responses:

- "I am confused about God" (25 percent).
- "I don't think about God in these situations" (16 percent).
- "I wonder if God cares" (11 percent).
- "I doubt God exists" (7 percent).
- "I am angry toward God" (5 percent).
- "I am resentful toward God" (3 percent).

"Every morning you should wake up in your bed and ask yourself: 'Can I believe it all again today?' No, better still, don't ask it till after you've read *The New York Times*, till after you've studied that daily record of the world's brokenness and corruption, which should always stand side by side with your Bible. Then ask yourself if you can believe in the Gospel of Jesus Christ again for that particular day. If your answer's always Yes, then you probably don't know what believing means. At least five times out of ten the answer should be No because the No is as important as the Yes, maybe more so. The No is what proves you're human in case you should ever doubt it. And then if some morning the answer happens to be really Yes, it should be a Yes that's choked with confession and tears and . . . great laughter."
—Frederick Buechner, *The Return of Ansel Gibbs*[2]

If God is supposed to deliver his people from harm, then why is God "late" sometimes? Even more so, why would God let the world become a place where suffering and natural disasters happen so readily?

There are some good reasons why we need to ask these hard questions. For starters, there aren't any easy answers here that will satisfy everyone. The less certain we are, the more we need to talk about this issue with trusted friends. However, we also need to ask this question because it's a big deal for many Christians, especially Christians sitting on the fence with their faith. People are already talking about it. It doesn't help anyone if we just say, "Trust God and don't worry about this!" As an expert at worrying, I can tell you that "worry" or concern about a matter like this isn't a button you can just switch off. Either Christianity has a response to the problem of pain or it doesn't. We will certainly need faith, especially with an issue like this. However, we do God a disservice if we act like the Bible has nothing to say to these pressing issues. In fact, our final reason for digging into these questions has everything to do with God.

We need to talk about suffering, pain, and evil because the Bible itself deals with these topics. The Psalms, Job, Jeremiah, the Gospels, Peter's epistles, and Paul's epistles all dive into these topics for us already. We're dealing with a topic that the Bible already confronts.

SAVED OR SLAUGHTERED?

My dad used to love reading Hebrews 11 to me. He called it the "hall of faith" with its extensive list of nearly every major Bible character who persevered by faith. I used to think that having faith in Jesus was a bit like a magical protection spell. Follow Jesus and you'll be prosperous, safe, and healthy for a long time. As I started to pay better attention to that passage, I saw something quite disturbing. Some of those who "persevered" by faith still suffered quite a lot. And there were some who were tortured or killed because of their faith. The list reads like a horror movie:

- faced jeers and flogging
- chained and imprisoned
- put to death by stoning
- sawed in two
- killed by the sword
- dressed in sheepskins and goatskins (I suspect that would be worse if you lived in a trendy place like New York or LA)
- left destitute
- persecuted
- mistreated (Don't all of these qualify as being mistreated?)
- wandered in deserts and mountains, living in caves and in holes in the ground

Can you imagine listing something like this at a youth rally and shouting, *"Who's stoked about following Jesus now?"*

I can see why we'd want to avoid a list like this. Who doesn't love to speak about victory in Jesus? In fact, my favorite hymn as a child was "Victory in Jesus." Everybody loves a winner. "O martyrdom in Jesus . . ." doesn't have the same ring to it. It's hard to talk about the suffering that could result from following Jesus. However, that is actually the very thing Jesus promised his disciples. True to his word, they were imprisoned and beaten shortly after Pentecost, and their response wasn't a collective, "Why me?" Mind you, they weren't *hoping* to be beaten. However, when it did happen, they compared themselves to Jesus rather than the wealthy and prosperous. In fact, they rejoiced that they'd been counted worthy of suffering for Christ (see Acts 5:12–42).

The hostility of the religious insiders of their day confirmed their place in the kingdom of God. If they weren't attacked, then they assumed they had much bigger problems—like fitting in with the very people who opposed Jesus. They weren't wondering why Jesus wasn't protecting them even though Jesus promised to be with them until the end of the age.

It doesn't really add up.

I think I have an idea of what they were thinking, but before I dare to go there, let's step back for a minute to look at our limitations with such a difficult topic.

THE PROBLEM OF TALKING ABOUT THE PROBLEM OF PAIN AND EVIL

When my grandfather passed away, I had just driven home for eleven hours straight from college. He died an hour after I arrived. I stumbled out of bed to sit by his side as he breathed his last. My family sat around him weeping. It was one of the most beautiful and terrible moments of my life. I wasn't ready to say good-bye to him. I'd just met a beautiful woman who I knew I'd marry one day, and she wouldn't be able to meet the man who had been a second father to me.

I turned to my Bible, and all I could think of was the book of Lamentations. A big book of sad seemed like the best option for a time like that. I turned to Lamentations 3, reading about Jeremiah's weeping over the destruction of Jerusalem. I zeroed in on verses 19–26:

> I remember my affliction and my wandering,
>> the bitterness and the gall.
> I well remember them,
>> and my soul is downcast within me.
> Yet this I call to mind
>> and therefore I have hope:
> Because of the LORD's great love we are not consumed,
>> for his compassions never fail.

> They are new every morning;
>   great is your faithfulness.
> I say to myself, "The LORD is my portion;
>   therefore I will wait for him."
> The LORD is good to those whose hope is in him,
>   to the one who seeks him;
> it is good to wait quietly
>   for the salvation of the LORD.

It was the perfect passage for that moment. It reminded me that God was indeed present in a dark time, and that this moment of death and loss wasn't the last word. I didn't understand why my grandfather had to leave this world just then, but Jeremiah's mourning captured the tension of despair and hope that I felt. In the years that followed, I returned to Lamentations 3 as a way of processing pain and suffering. I needed an explanation at that moment to help me make sense of the pain I felt. I grieved, but I needed to think about my grief.

Several years later, my grandmother passed away after a long struggle where her lungs gradually shut down. It was horrible to watch her decline,

---

Author and scholar C. S. Lewis was no stranger to grief and pain. After the death of his wife, he wrote the book *A Grief Observed*. Here are two of my favorite quotes:

> Not that I am (I think) in much danger of ceasing to believe in God. The real danger is of coming to believe such dreadful things about Him. The conclusion I dread is not "So there's no God after all," but "So this is what God's really like. Deceive yourself no longer."[3]

> We were promised sufferings. They were part of the program. We were even told, "Blessed are they that mourn," and I accept it. I've got nothing that I hadn't bargained for. Of course it is different when the thing happens to oneself, not to others, and in reality, not imagination.[4]

and I once again turned to Scripture when she passed away. I opened Lamentations 3, but this time something was different. I felt the sting of death, but there was something about Jeremiah's words about God's love in the midst of affliction that failed to speak to me. It felt like my old self was time traveling into the present to force an *explanation* on me that I wasn't ready to hear. Sometimes we don't need explanations. We just need to sit with our grief and know that God is present.

Why do some explanations work in one context and fail in another? Why do our attempts to explain the relationship of God and suffering come across as cold and unfeeling in one moment and perfectly reasonable in another?

I have a friend who is a brilliant psychologist. While discussing the problem of evil and pain in the world, he mentioned the difference between cold cognition and hot cognition.

Cold cognition is the more logical line of reasoning that isn't rooted in a particular situation. Since the matter isn't personal, you're free to dispassionately consider a variety of possible explanations. This chapter here is a chilly dose of cold cognition since I don't know you or your life circumstances. I hope I don't give you brain freeze.

Hot cognition is what we think about in the midst of a specific situation. The focus is more on experiencing heightened emotions and coping rather than critically examining all of the possibilities. The problem that many Christians run into is this: we sometimes dump a barrel of cold cognition onto heartbreaking and difficult situations that call for empathy and hot cognition. The person in the midst of suffering and pain doesn't want a chilly, logical explanation for pain and evil in the world. Important though these things may be to consider after the sting of the immediate moment passes, the pain of tragedy is hardly the place to have a lively chat about God's role in a world with pain.

When friends go through a really tough situation, they sometimes ask really tough questions in a moment of hot cognition. I may have a perfectly logical answer to this question, but I'm approaching the situation from a position of cold cognition. My cold answer may do more harm than good in a moment of hot cognition that requires empathy and presence. The same tension is all over the book of Job as his friends provide cold-cognition answers in the midst of his tremendous suffering.

For whatever reason, I really needed some time after my grandfather's death to process pain and suffering. I needed some answers. Perhaps I was just in a black-and-white phase of my life. However, when my grandmother passed away, I needed to grieve and feel her loss without resorting to an explanation from the Bible about things getting better somehow, someday.

Even on a more corporate level of national grief over a terrorist attack or one of America's many school shootings, a national tragedy calls for a compassionate reminder about the presence of God in the midst of suffering rather than an orderly argument about sin, suffering, and God. There may be a time for orderly answers, but explanations rarely help in the midst of immediate grief and loss.

Some aspects of this chapter may prove helpful when you're grieving with a friend. However, a great deal of this discussion about God's relationship with pain and suffering belongs in the realm of cold cognition and may not prove appropriate immediately after a personal tragedy. If you're feeling particularly raw after a deeply personal loss, it may be best to return to this chapter after you've had a chance to grieve a while longer. There's no rush. Healing takes time.

IS YOUR LIFE ALREADY MAPPED OUT?

The Bible often adds to our confusion about the level of God's involvement in our lives. On the one hand, the Bible makes it clear that God has a greater plan in the works that no one can stop. God also provides each person with specific gifts and talents. God is all powerful and able to make his plans come to pass. On the other hand, God regularly gives people choices, grieves the bad decisions of his people, and even lets people convince him to change his mind—as in Moses intervening on behalf of Israel. Different Christian traditions have their own explanations for these seeming discrepancies, and while I can't say I'll make everyone happy with what I offer up for consideration here, I think we'll find some surprising and extremely useful common ground that will help us sort out God's place in a world with pain and suffering.

What if God is both less involved in the course of our world than we suspected and far more involved than we would have ever imagined? All that is to ask, is it possible that God is involved in the world and individual lives in ways that we overlook?

There are many stories from Scripture that we could look at, but let's take a look at two that illustrate God's involvement in directing the course of the world and the role of free will.

In the creation story, God promised Eve that her offspring would one day crush the head of the serpent. There's no doubt in this story that God is predicting a future event that was intended to come to pass. God is powerful enough to ensure that this victory over Satan will happen. While we have seen the victory of Christ on the cross that fulfilled this prediction in part, we await the day when the Son of God fully destroys Satan and visibly rules the earth. In a sense, the course of history has been set. Evil will be defeated, and Christ will be Lord over all. This isn't a future that is up for grabs. God won't be surprised by the actions of Satan, and God certainly doesn't need our help to make sure he wins the final battle.[5]

As much as the course of history has been set, individual lives are a far more difficult matter to sort out in Scripture. On multiple occasions, God offers his people choices that lead to specific outcomes. While nothing they do can override God's larger plans for all of humanity or change the gifts he's given them, God offers people choices in their day-to-day lives.

For example, King Solomon was warned to remain obedient to the law or else his kingdom would crumble. While Solomon started out great, he eventually turned to false gods and made alliances with foreign kings rather than trusting in God. Solomon's disobedience signaled the end of Israel's golden age as the nation split in two after his reign. Solomon's failures, in part, brought about the Assyrian and Babylonian invasions since he allowed false gods to set up shop in the land.

I don't think God would play games with Solomon, setting the future in stone but "pretending" to give him a choice. Solomon had decisions to make, and he reaped the consequences. Each king who followed had the same options: follow God or do your own thing.

The story of Solomon and the kings who followed his reign is quite a downer, and that's why the New Testament presents us with such a fascinating turn of events at Pentecost. With the arrival of Pentecost, God imparts the Holy Spirit to his people—an event that God had long pointed toward. With the Spirit of God living among and even within God's people, we have a whole new take on the role of God in world events. God wants to be integrally involved in our decisions and to empower us to minister to others.

In other words, God may not direct every single event of our lives. God is not nudging us toward sins or harmful decisions. However, God is most certainly involved in guiding and directing us if we're open to it, and that direction certainly plays into God's larger plans that have been set in place. All that to say, God doesn't necessarily have to direct every little detail of our lives, but with the Holy Spirit among and within us, God is certainly capable of directing us in significant ways. It's a fuzzy, murky thing that we can't break down into a formula, but once we get a better handle on the ways God interacts with our world—relationally rather than through thunderbolts and mind control—we'll be in a better place to discuss pain and evil in our world.

DOES GOD DELIVER US FROM EVIL?

As the book of Hebrews suggests, God does not necessarily save his people from pain, suffering, and evil. We are promised that the Lord is a fortress and strong tower for those who put their trust in him, but at the same time, the Lord will not always protect his people from pain. The history of the martyrs from the early church should back up this point quite dramatically as well. Their security was in the future hope through the risen Jesus and the assurance of the resurrection, not deliverance from persecution.

I personally find that terrifying. I would really prefer that God use his power to save me from pain and suffering. Is God just sitting on his power? Is God indifferent? Is God not as powerful as we thought?

While there is plenty of mystery surrounding a topic like this, part of our difficulty in understanding it has to do with our ability to grasp the ways of God. If you're anything like me, you want to avoid danger and suffering. If I don't have to get involved in a mess, I won't go out of my way for

LEARNING TO LAMENT

We read in Ecclesiastes 7:2: "It is better to go to a house of mourning than to go to a house of feasting, for death is the destiny of everyone; the living should take this to heart."

That's a little on the heavy side, but Jesus followed this up with his teaching, "Blessed are those who mourn, for they will be comforted" (Matt. 5:4).

Scripture repeatedly encourages us to face our grief and to encounter it with others. In fact, mourning is inevitable in this world. Perhaps we need to dwell on the psalms of lament that teach us to present our difficulties to God, such as Psalm 5:3–4:

> In the morning, LORD, you hear my voice;
>   in the morning I lay my requests before you
>   and wait expectantly.
> For you are not a God who is pleased with wickedness;
>   with you, evil people are not welcome.

While suffering is a certainty in this life, it also isn't the final word at the close of history in the book of Revelation:

> And I heard a loud voice from the throne saying, "Look! God's dwelling place is now among the people, and he will dwell with them. They will be his people, and God himself will be with them and be their God. 'He will wipe every tear from their eyes. There will be no more death' or mourning or crying or pain, for the old order of things has passed away." (Rev. 21:3–4)

it. The mystery of Jesus is that he is fully God, and yet he chose to become a human being and suffer alongside us. Think of how Jesus is described in Philippians 2:6–8:

> Who, being in very nature God,
>   did not consider equality with God something to be
>   used to his own advantage;

rather, he made himself nothing
　　by taking the very nature of a servant,
　　being made in human likeness.
And being found in appearance as a man,
　　he humbled himself by becoming obedient to
　　death—even death on a cross!

Jesus was not cold, distant, and uninvolved in our world. He experienced pain, grief, and death alongside everyone else. That doesn't solve all of our problems with pain and suffering, but it tells us that God is involved in our world, identifies with us, and suffers alongside us. In fact, if the Holy Spirit has come to live inside of us, then God is deeply involved in our day-to-day trials as well.

Jesus didn't just go to earth on a field trip to see how the pitiful little humans were getting along. He suffered alongside his own people and then sent the Spirit of God to dwell among us in this world. Rather than imagining God sitting up in heaven with arms crossed and foot tapping, waiting for all of those stupid people to get their acts together, we can imagine God completely involved in the events of our lives each day, interacting with his people as they pray and read Scripture. God feels our disappointments, grief, and joy. If we're willing to open ourselves to the Spirit of God, we'll find that we can tap into the emotions of God as well, feeling God's sorrow over a friend's suffering or the elation of heaven over a relative who has received the gospel message for the first time.

The presence of the Holy Spirit means that God is deeply involved in our world today relationally through his people who continue to be the body of Christ on earth, but that doesn't necessarily solve all of our problems.

WHERE IS GOD DURING NATURAL DISASTERS?

One of the most disturbing ways I've heard anyone speak of God has to do with the ways God has been linked to natural disasters. Whether hurricanes, tornadoes, or earthquakes, it's typical for a fringe Christian pastor or ministry leader to make a remark that in some way links God to causing the disaster. Even so, our language tends to muddy the water regarding

God's involvement in a natural disaster, as we call them an "act of God" or say that it was the "hand of God."

Does God cause natural disasters?

The Bible certainly has stories where God used severe weather and earthquakes to intervene in human events, but does that demand the conclusion that God is orchestrating every single weather event?

While the Bible never states outright that God causes every single natural event, the Bible suggests that God has set things like our weather patterns

THE YEAR OF THE LORD'S FAVOR

When Jesus read from Isaiah 61, he announced that the hope of God's present rule had begun through his ministry, and we look forward to the complete fulfillment of this promise in the future. Take note of the justice that comes along with the comfort of God:

The Spirit of the Sovereign LORD is on me,
    because the LORD has anointed me
    to proclaim good news to the poor.
He has sent me to bind up the brokenhearted,
    to proclaim freedom for the captives
    and release from darkness for the prisoners,
to proclaim the year of the LORD's favor
    and the day of vengeance of our God,
to comfort all who mourn,
    and provide for those who grieve in Zion—
to bestow on them a crown of beauty
    instead of ashes,
the oil of joy
    instead of mourning,
and a garment of praise
    instead of a spirit of despair.
They will be called oaks of righteousness,
    a planting of the LORD
    for the display of his splendor.

(Isa. 61:1–3)

into place, causing rain to fall on the righteous and unrighteous, but not necessarily causing every single tornado and hurricane. In fact, when a tower fell on a group of people, Jesus rebuked his disciples for thinking that God had, in some way, sent the disaster as a form of judgment (Luke 13:4–5). However, Jesus' ability to calm a storm on the Sea of Galilee, let alone the story of Jonah, tells us that God has the power to intervene in nature.

For me, I find God's selective involvement in natural disasters to be the hardest to fathom. That God is powerful and yet supposedly stands by as natural disasters unfold leaves many of us confused and perhaps even angry. I certainly can't work my way toward an explanation at this point in my life.

However, there is one thing that gives me a lot of hope even in the midst of a perplexing topic like this. When Jesus returns to fully reveal his kingdom on earth, he will restore the earth, bringing about a new creation that removes the terror and chaos we experience in the natural world. When John notes in the book of Revelation that there will be no sea, he's making a symbolic statement about the lack of chaos and terror in the world. The sea was a place of danger and uncertainty in the ancient world, especially among the Jewish people. Just ask Paul how he felt about his shipwreck. The new creation won't kill off all of the sea creatures and dump a bunch of dirt into the oceans. The new creation will put an end to the chaos and terror that the oceans brought to the ancient mind. When God plans a perfect future, it's one without pain and suffering.

Whether or not we're disturbed by God's level of involvement in our world, the future we find in the Bible rights the wrongs we experience day by day. The kind of world we long for is the one that God is planning for all of eternity. That isn't to minimize the suffering and pain of this world. I can't fully explain that, and I'd be suspicious of anyone who can. However, I'm comforted to know that God feels the same way about this world as many of us, and he has a plan to do something about it.

A GOD PRESENT IN THE STORM

It has taken me a long time to accept that Jesus isn't here to solve all of my problems or to make my life easier. I don't like admitting that God is able to solve the world's problems but chooses to wait until the new creation.

However, as troubling as these points can be, God isn't distant from us. We have been given an inspired Bible that wrestles with these very questions for us, so we're in good company. In fact, I would suggest that God encourages us to ask these hard questions along with the saints from the past. God isn't trying to hide the hard parts from us. God even came to earth to experience them along with us.

I wish I could arrive at a more polished and complete "explanation" for the questions in this chapter. However, I sense that doing so wouldn't honor the complexity of this world and the many experiences people have with God and suffering.

The most comforting explanation I can find for God's relationship with pain and suffering is this brief verse of Scripture: "Jesus wept."

HELL

GETTING OUR GOATS . . . AND SHEEP

As A PUSHY YOUNG Christian, I spent a lot of time warning everyone I knew about the fires of hell because I didn't want anyone to go there. It was a perfectly logical step for a new believer in junior high. To my simple thinking, people just needed to be warned about hell in order to get them excited about following Jesus. If I could just present the problem, they would be falling over themselves for my solution. Right?

Unfortunately, the "bad news before the good news" approach resulted in a bunch of people just hearing the bad news and getting annoyed at me. No one at evangelism training warned me about this. The videos showed two women casually drinking tea in the kitchen, calmly talking about avoiding an eternity of torment in between sips of tea and nibbles on their low-fat cookies. I had no reason to doubt that every conversation about eternal hellfire goes exactly like that, which set me up for a rude awakening. To my surprise, most people aren't interested in talking once you've assured them of an eternity in the flames of hell.

Hell as eternal conscious torment causes all kinds of problems for Christians and non-Christians alike. It's often used to scare us into eternal life. It's also a major sticking point for many interested in salvation or those who find Jesus appealing but can't quite reconcile God with eternal torment. Maybe you've been a follower of Jesus for a long time and only recently began to struggle with the doctrine of hell. Then again, maybe you're deeply disturbed to hear that people would even think to call hell into question in the first place. Today's leading authors and theologians present a wide range of reactions.

In *Erasing Hell*, pastor Francis Chan implored his readers to take this topic superseriously and to pray extra hard that we'll have wisdom to get the details about hell extra super-duper right.[1]

Meanwhile, noted evangelical Christian theologian N. T. Wright is flat-out baffled that American Christians emphasize hell so much when we share the gospel, asking, "Why are Americans so fixated on hell?"[2]

In this chapter I'm going to play "devil's advocate." Some may argue that I'm literally taking the Devil's side on this issue. However, the rhetoric of all sides when it comes to hell can be pretty powerful. Those who support universalism say that anything less than universal salvation slanders the grace and mercy of God and turns God into a villain. Those who believe in annihilationism (the view that the damned are totally destroyed, also called conditional mortality) say the punishment of eternal hellfire hardly fits the crime of rejecting God in mortal life. Those who support a traditional view of hell as eternal conscious torment claim they're just taking the Bible at its word and any deviation from that can't take the heat that the Bible brings. Some add that a violation against God's eternal holiness even demands an eternal punishment. I also wonder if the eternal torment camp feels a need for eternal torture as a fitting counterpart for eternal life.

At stake here is the justice and mercy of God. Hell isn't just a problem for outsiders of our faith. It's a disturbing possibility that has troubled many Christians, especially those who became followers of Jesus to avoid an eternally fired-up fate.

IS ERASING HELL A MODERN TREND?

Christians arguing about the details of hell is nothing new in the history of the church. It just so happens that we've had renewed interest in debating the details of hell in the late twentieth and early twenty-first centuries. Theologians such as John Stott and Clark Pinnock have challenged the traditional conception of hell with their arguments for annihilation, along with popular preacher Rob Bell, the Beelzebub of devil's advocates who asks a megaton of questions. Even F. F. Bruce, who penned some of the most significant commentaries that pastors rely on today, chose to remain uncommitted on the question of hell.[3] C. S. Lewis offered a toned-down version of hell in *The Great Divorce*, downgrading the tormenting fires to a nondescript "grey town," and in *The Problem of Pain* he mused that the eternal fire of hell most likely speaks to finality, not duration.[4] Some would have us believe that we are living in a time that is unable to handle the truth of hell, as many are trying to "soften" our view of God. Nobody wants a big bad God who sends people to hell forever, right?

Well, it's not quite that simple.

In fact, several early church fathers advocated (or appear to have advocated) for annihilation, including Theophilus of Antioch[5] and Irenaeus.[6] Clement of Alexandria suggested that God will restore all things one day since the "fire" of judgment served the purpose of puri-fication, not punishment. In addition, something of a street fight exists among scholars regarding the views of Justin Martyr on this topic. At the very least he muddied the waters in one hotly debated passage from his *Dialogue with Trypho the Jew*.[7] If nothing else, Justin left open the possibility that God could save some outside the Christian faith. In fact, there are even debates about how to translate the writings of these church fathers in the first place before we even begin debating what these great thinkers had in mind. Regardless, if you read church history, you'll recognize that these are the good guys who helped shape early Christianity, and they are hardly unanimous. At the heart of their struggle was the philosophical and theological puzzle of their day about the nature of the human soul: could a mortal soul be "destroyed" for eternity? Nevertheless, plenty of significant church fathers advocated for eternal conscious torment, including the heavyweights Augustine and Aquinas.

There's no doubt that the "traditional" view of hell as eternal torment in fire caught on and became the norm. We could theorize that the "best theology" won. However, as the church assumed the power of excommuni-cation or declaring certain people "anathema" (cursed), we can't overlook the power that came to the church then as the virtual gatekeeper to hell. If you can declare that someone is going to suffer in hell for eternity, you

THEOLOGY WITH A LOT AT THE STAKE

Christians burned other Christians at the stake for years throughout Europe. While the Reformation heated things up quite a bit with the various challenges to papal authority and the use of indulgences to essentially pay one's way out of purgatory, the Catholic Church was already in the business of torching heretics.

Bible translator and early reformer John Wycliffe was sort of torched by the Catholic Church. He vigorously opposed the abuses of the Roman Church and completed a partial English translation of the Bible in the language of the people, but he died of a stroke before the church's authorities could light him up. Not to be trifled with, Catholic authorities declared Wycliffe a heretic, dug up his bones forty-four years later, and burned them.

possess a power that is unparalleled. There aren't very many incentives to give it up. That is, until more democratic forms of government and church leadership came along.

That isn't to say the traditional view of hell is wrong or that it's only the product of a conspiracy among the powerful. Rather, there weren't incentives or precedents for questioning it for many, many years. In fact, the church notoriously killed people who crossed it on doctrinal grounds. So you had to pick and choose your battles if you took issue with the church's theology. Hell wasn't the kind of doctrine someone would risk life and limb over, yet church authorities burned other dissenters for lesser offenses. Innovations such as indulgences took center stage instead when the Protestant Reformation spread across Europe.

Lastly, we need to keep in mind that this discussion of hell is not a universal concern among Christians. For example, the Eastern Orthodox Church isn't all that interested in debates over hell as a place of eternal torment. They have their own view where all of humanity is ushered into the presence of God upon death, but the wicked experience the light of God's presence as a torment and that's that. While the details of this debate are

important, we should remind ourselves that committed followers of Jesus
are all over the map on this topic.

NO ONE IS HAPPY ABOUT HELL

I can understand that someone may find it jarring to have any long-held
doctrine called into question. I went through something like that when
I learned that the Hebrew word we translate as "day" in Genesis 1 could
just as easily mean "period of time." I suddenly felt silly for fighting evolution for so many years. I was especially annoyed that my *Truth* fish (the
one that's eating a Darwin fish with legs) damaged the paint job on my
car when I peeled it off. However, in the case of hell, isn't it good news that
there are some alternative views to eternal conscious torment? I for one
would really like one of those alternatives to be correct, even if I'm bound
first and foremost to what I find in the Scriptures. And even if you believe
that God annihilates the wicked, that's still pretty terrible, right? If we
all agree that rejecting God brings serious consequences such as separation from God, do we really need to agree on the details of separation?
As we look at hell, I want to let the Scriptures speak and take them seriously, but I want to make it clear that I'm not approaching hell as a heresy
test. I believe there is room in the Christian family for a broad range of
perspectives on hell because the evidence isn't cut-and-dried. Rather than
advocating for one view, I find that my task is more a matter of examining
some possibilities that have been largely overlooked and asking some hard
questions, especially for the majority view of eternal conscious torment.

Before we talk about the possible details about hell in the Bible, let's
get a handle on a couple of boundary markers. For starters, discussing
the nature of hell is quite different from advocating universal salvation
for everyone. The topic of universal salvation is way beyond anything I
hope to address here. There are some church fathers who believed in the
possibility of God one day restoring all people to himself as well as some
scholars today who advance this view. However, I'd like to focus this chapter on the nature of God's judgment and what we can know about God's
punishment.

There is some common ground that we can all find in Scripture. Jesus
will judge sin and evil. Judgment is one of the most certain aspects of

Scripture. Hell on the other hand is far less clearly spelled out than many people may think it is or want it to be. That isn't to say that "everything you've ever heard about hell is wrong." Rather, the details surrounding hell in the Bible are quite complex, especially since we are so far removed from the culture and language of the Bible. Adding to the confusion, no one around today has gone to hell and back, so it's not like anyone can confirm a particular theory.

ARE WE TALKING ABOUT *SHEOL, GEHENNA,* OR *HADES?*

The Bible doesn't actually have one word that directly translates as "hell" per se. In fact, there isn't even a consistent concept throughout the Testaments for a specific place where eternal punishment takes place. If we were relying on the Old Testament, we wouldn't even have this conversation.

A REVIEW OF HELL 2.0 NT EDITION

The previous version of hell was imprecise and a bit clunky. The *Sheol* 1.0 version was a leader in its time when it came to containing those who departed from this life. However, it failed to provide a clear destination for the saved and the damned. These "errors" were first spotted during Second Temple Judaism (roughly 516 B.C.–A.D. 70) and then applied to the conception of hell in the New Testament. Hell 2.0 NT cranks up the temperature with a dose of everlasting fire for the wicked, replacing *Sheol*'s negative implications with a clearer picture of the destiny of many.

Nevertheless, the language programming bugs that plagued *Sheol* persist for some users who claim that Greek words such as *Hades* and *Gehenna* fail to paint a clear picture of the dark side of the afterlife. In addition, the use of "everlasting fire" brings up translation debates about the precise meaning of the word "everlasting" in this context. A future release is not expected, and therefore continued usage of Hell 2.0 NT edition will continue to cause program crashes and lengthy debates among theological programmers.

The Old Testament has a kind of holding tank for the dead called *Sheol*.[8] Everyone died and went to *Sheol*. This was simply where all the departed go, or it simply designated their disembodied condition in a netherworld called *Sheol*. We never get the impression that only bad things happened there or that the wicked went to a different, possibly hotter, section of it. Hell as we know it most likely first took shape during the period between the Testaments when the Jews suffered persecution and even death at the hands of Samaritan, Greek, and Roman enemies. It's an understandable development. With the brief exception of a successful revolt under Judas Maccabeus, the Jewish people didn't have much to cheer about after their return from exile. From the appearance of things, the Gentiles were winning and proving that their gods were superior. The Jews' only theological explanation for their circumstances was, "Just you wait until the day of the Lord." Gentile victory in this life was only a temporary state of affairs. God's judgment would topple their enemies one day, just not "today."

If you want to bring down the mood in a party, just read a bit of *1 Enoch*, a book that resembles the book of Revelation in a number of ways (more on that in the "end of the world" chapter). Enoch's author has some particularly heavy descriptions of judgment scenes such as this one: "Then Uriel, one of the holy angels who was with me, answered and said: 'This accursed valley is for those who are accursed for ever: Here shall all the accursed be gathered together who utter with their lips against the Lord unseemly words and of His glory speak hard things'" (*1 Enoch* 27:2).[9] Some believe this valley is the same as the Hinnon Valley, which later became known as "*Gehenna*."[10] Whether or not that's the case, Enoch's point is that God will one day bring down judgment on those who oppose him, and that judgment, either symbolically or literally, will take place in a valley.

When Jesus hit the scene we see a more defined picture of the afterlife with a heaven and a place of punishment that follows the lead of Enoch and other contemporary Jewish authors. However, he doesn't use the word "hell" per se. He picks up the existing tradition of "*Gehenna*," which some believe was a garbage dump outside the city of Jerusalem at the time of Christ. Others focus on the valley's association with child sacrifices during the time of the kingdom of Judah—acts that linked it with God's coming judgment (2 Kings 23:10; Jer. 7:31; 32:35). There's also a possibility that *Gehenna* took on a more immediate meaning of God's judgment as an imminent event, as some Jews at the time of Jesus no doubt believed that the day of the Lord or day of God's judgment could happen at any moment. *Gehenna* had a reputation as a place of burning and evil. There's no doubt that this created a powerful image of being left out of God's presence, but it's quite another matter to determine how literal we should take these images. In the immediate context of Jesus, we can't even say that there was a consensus among his audience.

How often did Jesus actually talk about hell? I have heard plenty of Bible teachers say that Jesus talked about hell a lot. However, many of the references we have are repeats. Here's a brief overview with the repeat passages omitted but noted:

Instance 1: Slander

> Matthew 5:22: "And anyone who says, 'You fool!' will be in danger of the fire of *Gehenna*."[11]

Instance 2: "Better Than" Sayings

> Matthew 5:29: "It is better for you to lose one part of your body than for your whole body to be thrown into *Gehenna*."
> Matthew 5:30: "It is better for you to lose one part of your body than for your whole body to go into *Gehenna*."
> Matthew 18:9: "It is better for you to enter life with one eye than to have two eyes and be thrown into the fire of *Gehenna*."
> Note: All three "better than" sayings are repeated in Mark 9:43–47.

Instance 3: Fear God Alone

> Matthew 10:28: "Do not be afraid of those who kill the body but cannot kill the soul. Rather, be afraid of the One who can destroy both soul and body in *Gehenna*."
> Note: This saying is repeated in Luke 12:5.

Instance 4: Woe Sayings

> Matthew 23:15: "Woe to you, teachers of the law and Pharisees, you hypocrites! You travel over land and sea to win a single convert, and when you have succeeded, you make them twice as much a child of *Gehenna* as you are."

Matthew 23:33 (to the teachers of the law and Pharisees): "You snakes! You brood of vipers! How will you escape being condemned to *Gehenna?*"

Gehenna most often comes up as a place that is outside of God's kingdom. *Gehenna* was the place where those who resisted God's teachings or who remained committed to their own way of living would be cast into. It's a place where God throws people, and there's one mention in Mark 9:43 that *Gehenna* is an everlasting fire: "It is better for you to enter life maimed than with two hands to go into *Gehenna*, where *the fire never goes out*" (emphasis added). That last phrase of the verse is translated "unquenchable fire" in a couple of similar passages (see Matt. 3:12; Luke 3:17). The idea in Mark 9:43 is that the fire itself is unstoppable or even eternal. This fiery image shows up in Jesus' parable about the Son of Man when he comes in his glory and separates people on the basis of their relationship to him, even as a shepherd separates sheep from goats: "Then he will say to those on his left [the goats], 'Depart from me, you who are cursed, into *the eternal fire* prepared for the devil and his angels'" (Matt. 25:41, emphasis added). As a matter of fact, the unquenchable fire of Mark 9:43 paired with the everlasting fire of Matthew 25:41 may provide the most convincing argument for hell as a place of eternal torment. Nevertheless, some argue that those who choose the path that leads to "eternal fire" over "eternal life" cannot burn forever since they are logically unable to "exist forever." The waters are further muddied by Bible commentator William Barclay who argued that the punishment described in this passage, summed up with the Greek word *kolasis* in Matthew 25:46, is remedial (ultimately restorative), as the word was often used to describe pruning.[12] Our interpretations hinge on how we interpret these Greek phrases that we approximate as "eternal fire," "unquenchable fire," and "eternal punishment" from the distance of nearly two thousand years.

If *Gehenna* is a place of eternal burning and punishment where an unbelieving person is sent as a consequence of rejecting his message, Jesus didn't exactly drive home the importance of this in his final instructions to his disciples. He focused more on the kingdom of God and on making disciples. Any connections we make about *Gehenna* depend on a few verses where we have to interpret the meaning of a Jewish symbol of judgment and weigh the meaning of "eternal fire." I'm not saying that hell as a place of eternal conscious torment is impossible. I'm just saying that I sure wish he'd been a bit clearer about it. Interpreting Jesus' teaching on hell is difficult not because we don't want to see the clear truth. It's because we are so far removed from the symbols and imagery of his day that it's hard to arrive at a definite conclusion.

The rest of the New Testament doesn't clear things up as much as we'd hope. In fact, the images of *Gehenna* fade away in the Epistles, as each writer tended to focus more on the fact that judgment is coming than on giving a description of hell itself. Having said that, Paul, Peter, and John had no problem with speaking of certain people being cut off from Christ or condemned. Paul told Timothy that the sins of some are obvious and that judgment surely awaits them (1 Tim. 5:24), which isn't exactly an affirmation of hell, but it suggests that God's judgment is coming to some. The author of Hebrews has a far more sobering warning for the believers: "If we deliberately keep on sinning after we have received the knowledge of the truth, no sacrifice for sins is left, but only a fearful expectation of judgment and of raging fire that will consume the enemies of God" (Heb. 10:26–27). Outside of the Gospels, James alone uses the term *Gehenna* and names it as the source that ignites that small and inflammatory organ of the body that every human being finds so difficult to control: "The tongue also is a fire, a world of evil among the parts of the body. It corrupts the whole body, sets the whole course of one's life on fire, and is itself set on fire by *Gehenna*" (James 3:6). So far, in the Epistles we've got judgment and a "consuming fire" that sets people's tongues ablaze. Check.

As we would suspect, fiery old Peter isn't afraid to confront the high-stakes issue of hell as well. After explaining the various ways God had judged the wicked and delivered people like Noah and Lot in the past, he wrote, "If this is so, then the Lord knows how to rescue the godly from trials and to hold the unrighteous for punishment on the day of judgment. This is especially true of those who follow the corrupt desire of the flesh and despise authority" (2 Peter 2:9–10). So those consumed with sin will be judged. Peter also penned the ever cheerful, "By the same word the present heavens and earth are reserved for fire, being kept for the day of judgment and destruction of the ungodly" (2 Peter 3:7). Besides punishment

WILL WE EVER AGREE ON HELL?

Noted New Testament scholar F. F. Bruce remained publicly uncommitted on the topic of hell. In the foreword of Edward Fudge's *The Fire That Consumes*, he wrote,

> If there is no unanimity here among people who are agreed in accepting the Bible as their rule of faith, it may be inferred that the biblical evidence is not unambiguous. In such a situation polemic should have no place. What is called for, rather, is the fellowship of patient Bible study.[13]

on the day of judgment, the ungodly will be destroyed. These verses paint a bleak future for the ungodly, but they aren't exactly eternal conscious torment.

In Jude 7 we run into "eternal fire" again. However, if we look at the context, Jude would be making a strange comparison if he really had "eternal fire" in mind when he described the destruction of Sodom and Gomorrah: "They serve as an example of those who suffer the punishment of eternal fire." Cities destroyed in a historical event certainly aren't still burning today, although the fire that destroyed them was definitive, bringing everlasting consequences. That hints that the word we translate as "eternal" may have some other meanings we need to talk about.

And then there's the interpretive black hole that is the book of Revelation.

Before we place too much stock in anything we find in Revelation for the topic of hell, let's step back for a moment and consider that the interpretation of Revelation is a highly contentious matter. Some scholars place it primarily in the first century, describing the struggles of the early church at the hands of the Roman Empire. Others see the book as symbolic of present and future events. And still others locate the events of Revelation in a dystopian future that turns the book's imagery into a timeline of future events. Into this contentious mess we can now stand on the shores of the lake of fire and "dive in" as it were.

On the one hand, the Devil, the Beast, and the False Prophet will be tossed into the lake of fire where they will be tormented day and night (Rev. 20:10). We don't know for certain how literally to read this. Does the lake of fire stand for a form of judgment or is it a literal place? There's no way we can know for certain, but we do know one particular detail: these three are the only characters who are said to be tortured for eternity in the lake of fire. At the white throne judgment, anyone whose name is not found in the Book of Life is also cast into the lake of fire where such people suffer the second death. There is no mention of them being tormented day and night (Rev. 20:14–15). The point is that they die a second time instead of being raised to life. Some have even suggested that the phrase "second death" indicates that conscious torment for eternity is impossible if you've just died again.

Examining the use of the word *Hades*[14] in the New Testament offers a few twists and a more substantive picture than *Gehenna*. Jesus said that Capernaum will "go down to *Hades*" (Matt. 11:23), the gates of *Hades* will not prevail against the church (Matt. 16:18), and the rich man in the parable about he and Lazarus was tormented in *Hades* (Luke 16:23). *Hades* also gives up its dead in the book of Revelation for the final judgment. Is *Hades* the closest thing we can find to a notion of hell as a place of eternal torment?

That's possible, but the second-century-B.C. Jews who translated the Old Testament into Koine Greek (the language also used for the New Testament) rendered the Hebrew word *Sheol* as *Hades* in the Septuagint. So *Hades* as used in the Greek Old Testament referred to the realm of the dead given its use as a synonym for *Sheol* in the Hebrew Bible, but in the New Testament the term *Hades* was used more specifically to designate the place where the damned are tormented. It's clear that there are some extremely negative associations with *Hades* in the New Testament as we've noted. The people of Capernaum don't want to be cast into *Hades*, Peter doesn't want the gates of *Hades* to prevail, and in Jesus' parable the rich man wanted nothing more than to escape *Hades*. When John writes in Revelation that *Hades* itself will be destroyed, it's worth asking whether we should kiss our arguments over *Hades* good-bye since it's not an eternal location in the first place (Rev. 20:14). It's clear that *Hades* (like *Sheol*) is some kind of holding place for the dead, and whether or not we associate it with a notion of hell as "eternal torment," we run into a dead end of sorts with its destruction in the lake of fire.

I hope you can feel the tension at play in Scripture when it comes to the topic of hell. Cases can be made for several perspectives based on Scripture, but we're all dealing with the same limitations: distance from the symbols and definitions of the Bible's writers and our own preconceptions.

KILLING THE DEAD AGAIN . . . AND AGAIN

So let's try to add up what we know and what we don't know about hell. According to the Bible, there is some kind of existence after death in *Sheol/ Hades*, heaven, or *Gehenna*. Death is not the end for us. According to the New Testament, there are two destinations. Some are welcomed into God's presence and others are cast outside of it. There is mention of "eternal fire" in several verses, but we don't know for certain whether an "eternal fire" or "unquenchable fire" means that those cast into the fire will also be tormented eternally (the fire itself is eternal/unquenchable), but that may or may not apply to those in the fire. In addition, *Hades* itself will be thrown into the lake of fire (Rev. 20:14). The notion of eternal fire is far from a major focus throughout the commissioning of the apostles, the preaching in the book of Acts, and the Epistles. In addition to the mentions of "eternal fire," the Bible also uses words such as "eternal destruction" and "second death" to describe the fate of those who fall under God's judgment. "Eternal fire" could line up quite logically with all of the Bible's talk about the destruction of the wicked.

Now let's add up what we don't know for sure.

While Jesus certainly speaks about *Gehenna*, casting some out of God's presence, and "eternal fire" (on two occasions), he wasn't exactly explicit about describing hell as we've come to know it, even if there are some key details such as judgment and separation from God. In addition, "eternal fire" or "eternal destruction" does not demand an eternal conscious torment that goes on and on—it may well be eternal in the sense of finality. If eternal hellfire is really on the line, that strikes me as something that Jesus and the disciples would want to spell out. Isn't an eternity in hell a really big deal? That isn't to say that unending, everlasting torment in fire isn't possible based on the biblical witness. There's no doubt that argument can be made. However, there's enough ambiguity associated with the terms used that we can have a rather lively debate.

DO WE NEED HELL?

While we need to carefully weigh the traditions passed down to us about hell, we also need to ask whether our traditions have made assumptions based on the witness of Scripture. This wouldn't be the first time the church has asked such questions—hello Reformation and Abolition movement.

I find it most helpful to start with the essential thing that we need from a holy and loving God: justice. Justice is woven throughout the Scriptures. The righteous gave justice to the poor and powerless, while the "wicked" were typically exploiting others and violating the commands of God. The necessary partner to justice is judgment. We need God to determine what we deserve, and we expect God to judge those who persist in doing evil. The point of Scripture time and time again is that God will judge evil and bring justice to our world. Whether or not "hell" as an "eternal location" plays a part in that judgment, justice is our main point of contention. On

WHO GOES TO HEAVEN?

There is no doubt throughout the Old Testament that YHWH is the only God and throughout the New Testament that Jesus alone saves. However, Matthew 25:37–40 suggests that we may be surprised at who is saved on Judgment Day:

> Then the righteous will answer him, "Lord, when did we see you hungry and feed you, or thirsty and give you something to drink? When did we see you a stranger and invite you in, or needing clothes and clothe you? When did we see you sick or in prison and go to visit you?"
> The King will reply, "Truly I tell you, whatever you did for one of the least of these brothers and sisters of mine, you did for me."

this point N. T. Wright adds, "Reason itself may perhaps suggest that, if God is indeed to put the world to rights, and if he has indeed given his human creatures the freedom we sense ourselves to have, including the freedom to reject his will and his way, the eventual judgment will involve the loss of those who have exercised that freedom to their own ultimate cost."[15] In other words, God will give us what we desire.

A just God who judges those who do evil is not a soft, anything-goes God. However, if you struggle to accept a God who punishes people with eternal hellfire, there are some good reasons to hang on to the Christian faith. The Scriptures demand a just God who punishes evil, but they are far more uncertain about the details of that punishment than many people may realize or are willing to admit, including many devoted Christians.

On the other hand, if you are convinced that God punishes people with eternal hellfire, I wonder if you could ask yourself this question: Why do I need eternal hell to exist?

As I've wrestled with this doctrine, I've asked myself, Is it not enough to agree that God is just and will punish the unrepentant, and that we'll never know the details about hell in this life?

Misunderstanding hell could misrepresent God and dramatically change the stakes for those who reject the gospel. It has been a sticking point for many would-be converts to the Christian faith. While we can assert that hell may not be as bad as we thought, even a "downgrade" from eternal hellfire to annihilation still makes the concept of hell terrible.

The uncertainty surrounding the judgment of God has helped me rethink how I talk about the gospel. I'm not afraid to talk about separation from God or the possibility of hell, but I don't talk about it in the same way as when I was pushing fire and brimstone. The kingdom of God is bringing peace and restoration, and we don't want to miss it. We are offering God's peace and restoration, the antithesis of hell. There are still two paths set before us, one that leads to God and one that leads to chaos, pain, and even some kind of destruction apart from him. I don't focus on the details of that path apart from God because I'm not all that sure about the details anymore.

Jesus told his listeners to repent for the kingdom of God was near, not the fires of hell. We know that no one wants to end up in hell, but the focus of the Gospels is that God has something so wonderful for us that we don't want to miss out on it. If we're stuck debating the details of hell, then perhaps we should follow the lead of Jesus and spend more time talking about the kingdom of God and how it repairs the evil and destruction we witness around us every day.

ERRORS IN THE BIBLE?

FACT-CHECKING THE HOLY SPIRIT

THERE AREN'T TOO many times I can say, "PBS shocked me."

Classical music concerts? Zzzzz

The guy painting happy trees? I'll give him a minute or two.

Sesame Street? I already know to how to get there.

One evening I happened upon a special about Jesus. Perhaps my grandfather had it on. They had fantastic video footage of the land of Israel, and it caught my attention long enough that I listened in. While cameras panned the major sites in the land of Israel, a scholar provided a voice-over where he made astonishing claims like this: "We're certain that most of the New Testament was a fabrication of the early church."

Cue the record scratch.

He seemed so sure of himself, but his claim sounded like madness. Who would think of saying such a thing? How could this be? I'd always been taught that the Bible was reliable. As it turned out in the years that followed, remixing Jesus has become a major field of academic study.

"JESUS" IS HISTORY

You may have heard of the "Jesus Seminar" or "the historical Jesus" or perhaps you've stumbled upon a television show or book suggesting that

Jesus isn't who we all thought he was. The theories about the true, historical Jesus range from the partially helpful to looney-toon absurdity. We have certainly learned a lot more about the context of Jesus in the past two to three hundred years thanks to the findings of archaeology and a deeper study of Jewish literature from the time of Christ. Scholars who may not even identify themselves as Christians have made some of the best leaps forward.

Thanks to some of these scholars, we understand that Jesus thought of himself as a prophet announcing the imminent return of God and that the return from exile was an essential backdrop to his message. However, many of these scholars have also taken scissors to the Bible, picking and choosing which passages are "authentically" from Jesus and which were added later by the church. Some suggest he was a cynical teacher of pithy sayings and others suggest, à la *Jesus Christ Superstar*, that Judas is really the hero of the Gospels who was framed by a pouty and slightly crazy Jesus.

Phew! That's a lot to process. However, if you've ever encountered any of this, it can be quite disconcerting to be told that you may have been duped and put all of your trust in a fraud. If you're like me, you've made major life decisions because you believe God was leading you in one way or another to imitate Jesus as found in the Gospels. Every follower of Jesus is trusting in the hope of the resurrection and a future life with God. Nothing could be more catastrophic than learning the Gospels and much of the New Testament are merely fabrications.

Before we discuss our survival options, we need to dig a little deeper into how we approach these challengers of the historical Bible.

HOW "TRUE" MUST THE BIBLE BE?

A young man from Kansas enrolled in classes at Moody Bible Institute and then at Wheaton College in order to study the biblical languages. Passionate about Christianity and a champion debater, he dug deeper into the field of textual criticism at Princeton Seminary, a field that explores the history of the Bible's transmission and the manuscripts available in different regions of the world and at different points in time. He had learned to rely on the Bible as the foundation for his faith as a Christian and fully trusted that the Bible was completely free from errors. As he set about studying the Bible and the history of its transmission, he uncovered some disturbing details.

In particular, this young man found that the history of the Bible was filled with political intrigue and intense debates over manuscript variations. The more he uncovered the conflicts surrounding the origins of the Bible, the more he began to doubt the reliability of the Bible. In fact, he even found major discrepancies between the various textual versions. While textual variations are nothing new for students of the Bible (anybody who studied New Testament Greek knows about that), this young biblical scholar began to make a public case against the reliability of the Bible based on these variations. He believed that many of the differences were related to competing theological agendas within the church, and there was no telling whether the Bible we have today actually reflects the historical Jesus.

HOW RELIABLE ARE THE MANUSCRIPTS WE HAVE?

One of the earliest manuscripts we have of Paul's letters is known as Papyrus 46, or P46, that is conservatively dated between A.D. 150 and 200[1] and may even be earlier. This manuscript contains large portions of Paul's letters to the Romans, Corinthians, Ephesians, Galatians, Philippians, Colossians, and Thessalonians. It also contains the epistle to the Hebrews.

In fact, we currently have eighteen manuscripts dated between A.D. 100 and A.D. 200 and one manuscript containing the gospel of Mark that is dated before A.D. 100, altogether providing early manuscripts for about 43 percent of the New Testament. Greek scholar Daniel Wallace says that we have yet to find a significant deviation as each new papyrus is discovered. He writes, "As with all the previously published New Testament papyri (127 of them, published in the last 116 years), not a single new reading has commended itself as authentic. Instead, the papyri function to confirm what New Testament scholars have already thought was the original wording or, in some cases, to confirm an alternate reading—but one that is already found in the manuscripts."[2]

This scholar is Dr. Bart Ehrman, currently the James A. Gray Distinguished Professor at the University of North Carolina at Chapel Hill.

Ehrman is one of the most obvious examples of the pitfalls of making the Bible the primary foundation for Christianity. Once he found out just how hotly debated the origins of the Bible were, he bailed on Christianity.

I don't blame him. His reasoning is completely sound. He'd been raised in a Christian culture where the truthfulness of Christianity and his own faith rested completely in a book. Once that book came under fire, his faith did as well. He's not the only former Christian I know who has followed this course.

THE RIGHTEOUS SHALL LIVE BY THE BIBLE'S RELIABILITY?

We'll talk about the truthfulness of the Bible in a minute, but we need to start with a more basic question: What is the foundation for the Christian faith?

Many have made the Bible their foundation. Just look at doctrinal statements for ministries and churches that list the Bible in the top slot today. It's also historically true that many conservative Bible scholars in the late 1800s and early 1900s made a purely error-free Bible the foundation of their faith (taking things up a notch from "inspired by the Holy Spirit") in response to liberal scholars who focused more on "religious experiences" and saw the Bible as a collection of religious myths.

However, the problem with all of this is that we're supposed to have a different foundation for our faith. It's OK to say the Sunday school answer here since it's correct: Jesus. Paul wrote, "No one can lay any foundation other than the one already laid, which is Jesus Christ" (1 Cor. 3:11). Jesus is our foundation.

Granted, we need the stories about Jesus in the Gospels to be true and reliable. However, the living, risen person of Christ is the foundation for our faith. The Bible comes to life for us because the Holy Spirit is guiding us into the truth. We know the Father because he has drawn us to himself. God, the Father, Son, and Holy Spirit, is the reason why we can even find salvation in the words of Scripture in the first place. You could call it a chicken-and-egg issue, but the starting point for every major character in Scripture is an experience of the living God.

Abraham met God in the dusty wilderness of Israel.

Jacob literally wrestled with God.

Joseph found God in his dreams.

Samuel needed three tries before he met God.

Jesus knocked Paul off his feet.

While we have good reasons to affirm the truth of Scripture, we need to make sure we're affirming it for the right reasons. The Bible is important, but it isn't Jesus. Last I checked, no one says, "The Bible saves."

Part of what drove a person like Bart Ehrman away from the Christian faith was the belief that any doubts about the Bible render the entire Christian faith a fraud. This is the wrong battle. The battle isn't whether we can prove Christianity true through affirming every detail in the Bible. The battle is between Christ and sin, beginning with the incarnation and ending with the victory of the cross and resurrection. In these events, we find the life of God and the truth of the gospel.

We can affirm the Bible because it is true and testifies to these events, but Christianity is not built on "Scripture alone." We can affirm the historicity of Scripture without replacing Jesus as our one and only foundation. When a scholar calls our faith into doubt based on the Bible, our first response, though not our only response, is that we know the Bible is true because of what Christ has done in our lives and in the lives of others. The Spirit of the risen Lord is dwelling among us today. We can still dispute such claims by these scholars, but the most important truth of the Bible is the way it points us to new life in Christ. Scripture points us to Christ alone, testifying concerning him, the living Word of God who was in the beginning, the truth and the life.

CAN WE PROVE THAT THE BIBLE IS RELIABLE?

A guy like Bart Ehrman has a lot of advantages over most of us. He is a champion debater after all and has spent far more hours studying the Bible than most Christians. He used to be one of us, but he has defected after reviewing the evidence for the reliability of the Bible. This is the kind of stuff that can make Christians weak in the knees.

Can we stand up to a guy like Ehrman or his fellow scholars who cast doubt on the Bible? I can't guarantee a clear victory here, but I think I can help your weak, knocking knees.

Whom Will We Believe?

Part of the problem with a scholar like Ehrman is that we have to decide whom we're going to believe. We may well end up looking at the same evidence and arriving at different conclusions. This happens all of the time in every single academic discipline. We have brilliant economists who will fight tooth and nail over conservative vs. liberal economic policies. We have sociologists who arrive at different conclusions about trends in America based on the same data sets. We also have historians who sharply disagree about events in the recent past. Just look at the contentious debate among American historians over the cause of the American Civil War. Some suggest that it was based on states' rights, while others suggest that it's absurd to overlook slavery as the cause of the war.

COULD WE BE WRONG?

When we encounter someone who calls into question our deeply held beliefs, our first emotion is to go on the defensive. We don't like being wrong in general, but especially when it comes to our religious beliefs. In fact, journalist Kathryn Schulz, author of *Being Wrong*, suggests that once you "realize" that you're wrong about something, you feel embarrassed. However, being wrong is difficult to admit. "Being wrong doesn't feel like anything," she says in her TED Talk. We learn early in our lives that we don't want to be wrong, so we work hard to never be wrong. Sometimes we have to face potential embarrassment and uncertainty when asking tough questions about our deeply treasured beliefs. It's an unpleasant process, but it ensures that our confidence is in the right place.

This is not the first or last time that bright scholars have disagreed about historical evidence, especially when it comes to ancient history. If we can't agree about the Civil War, an event that was exceptionally well documented, what makes us think we'll arrive at some kind of consensus over Jesus? For instance, Ehrman is critical of the oral transmission method related to the early gospels. He compares oral transmission of ancient stories to the telephone game at a party where the original message becomes so distorted and ridiculous by the time it returns to the starting point, it is virtually unintelligible and useless.[5]

Call me nitpicky, but a party game doesn't compare all that well to communicating the life-changing message of a long-awaited, resurrected Messiah. The Jewish people waited centuries for the arrival of the Messiah. Their lives revolved around this anticipated event. If teenagers today still play the telephone game (something I doubt since they're all busy texting on their cell phones), there's a 99.9 percent chance that they're sharing a message that isn't quite as important as a Messiah who will liberate your nation from the crushing oppression of a foreign army.

Such a criticism of oral transmission is understandable in today's culture that relies on written texts and archived websites to capture ideas and to convey them accurately. Our culture rarely values the memorization of anything. The last thing I was forced to memorize was the Pledge of Allegiance in elementary school. Some professional singers forget the words to "The Star-Spangled Banner" at sports games. Speaking for Americans, we undoubtedly get an F for our ability to memorize anything.

However, one could argue that the oral transmission culture at the time of Jesus ensured that his story was actually preserved more accurately than with written documents.

How so?

For starters, just about every Jewish child memorized the first five books of the Old Testament.[6] Can you imagine how involved that must have been? I can understand memorizing Genesis and part of Exodus, but they also had to power through Leviticus and Numbers. That's a lot of ephods, measurements, and archaic names to remember. And more than that, many Jews committed the Psalms and portions of the Prophets to memory. When Jesus and his disciples rattled off Scripture quotations, they didn't have a scroll stuffed in their robes with handy Scripture verses on them. They memorized the Scriptures—lots and lots of Scriptures. Memorizing a gospel or two wasn't a big deal for the early church. Some theorize that the gospel of Mark was written in an easily memorized style. I can understand that we can't quite wrap our brains around this, but community-backed testimonies actually meant a lot more than a written document that could have been forged. In fact, forged documents were quite common back then. Remember that Paul even went so far as signing his own name at the end of one of his letters to prove its authenticity. It was far more important to maintain oral traditions within tight-knit communities where the stories could be fact-checked by other community members.

While it would be convenient to have a Roman imprint of a major publisher around in Palestine with an editorial review board and fact-checkers to review the process for the writing and collection of the Scriptures, we'll have to settle for the oral community method that was the way they did things back then. To suggest that people didn't care about getting the facts right or couldn't keep track of the details in an oral culture smacks of modern arrogance toward another time that we don't understand. This was far from the telephone game.

Jesus is calling, and the connection is just fine.

What Would You Die For?

If the Bible really was a disputed fabrication that we can't be certain about today, we need to look at the events surrounding its writing and transmission. I want to see the kinds of lives we find among the early church around the time the Bible was written and then passed down amid controversy, intrigue, and heresy leading up to the councils in the A.D. 300s and 400s that solidified the list of biblical books.

We can't deny the controversy and the political scheming that occurred. There's no doubt that we have some differences among the various manuscripts passed down to us. Every scholar of Christian history, conservative or liberal, agrees on these points. However, I find it helpful to ask what the early church was willing to do for the sake of their beliefs about the risen Jesus. On the whole, many Christians who believed in the literal incarnation, death, and resurrection of Jesus were willing to suffer persecution, loss of property, and even death for the sake of Christ.

GLADIATORS FOR JESUS

We hear about "martyrs" today who sacrifice themselves by launching terrorist attacks to kill other people. However, that sense of martyrdom is quite different from the early Christians who willingly surrendered their lives during the brutal persecutions carried out by Rome. These followers of Jesus surrendered themselves to be killed in the gladiator games and by other means of torture as a way of proving their commitment to Christ alone rather than fighting to preserve themselves.

Saint Anthony of the Desert (ca. 251–356), one of the earliest desert fathers in Egypt, ventured into a nearby city only when he learned that the ruler had been martyring Christians. When the magistrate learned of Anthony's boldness, he backed down, allowing the revered holy man to live. Anthony supposedly sulked back to his cave.

If Nero is nailing your friends and family to crosses, covering them in tar, and then torching them in his garden, you better believe the majority of Christians would *run* to the palace shouting, "We made it up! Really! The disciples stole his body from the tomb because they wanted to keep it going, but we're done with Jesus now! We're awesome at worshipping Caesar!"

At the start of the early church, there were Jews like Saul (later called Paul) who lead the charge in arresting and imprisoning Christians, and when they were executed, he voted against them. Even from the beginning, many Christians were willing to die for the sake of Christ. Remember, the main reason why Christianity spread was because people were killing them and they were running for their lives. While it's possible that someone may be deceived about a religious leader and be willing to die for him, many of the people who were dying in the early church were original eyewitnesses to the ministry of Jesus. That they suffered martyrdom tells me something: they knew the stories they passed along were true and worth dying for.

What Would You Record?

Critics of the Bible's historicity make a case that the authors and guardians of the Bible had an agenda, and these authors and editors changed the events they recorded in order to tell their own version of history. I can understand that line of reasoning, and I understand that the history of manuscripts is a tricky field that few of us fully understand. However, there's something about the Bible, the New Testament in particular, that suggests it's more truthful than some scholars today would expect.

If the writers and editors of the New Testament had an agenda, wouldn't you expect them to make "their guys" look as good as possible? If you have an agenda to promote, why would you "invent" or transmit stories that make Peter into a traitor, James and John into bloodthirsty brigands, and all the disciples into selfish Jewish patriots who barely understood Jesus and could only think of getting a throne in heaven? Oh, then there's Paul, the murderer of Christians who converted because of a mystical light. Good one! If you wanted to find damning evidence to discredit the disciples of Jesus and the stories they told, the New Testament will provide all that you need.

That line of reasoning doesn't resolve every qualm over the reliability of the Bible, but we can make a reasonable conjecture that anyone with an agenda would have omitted quite a few of the stories passed down to us. The Gospels end with stories of the disciples running away, hiding in upper rooms, and standing on a hillside, dazed and confused about why Jesus is flying away from them rather than building them a bunch of thrones. If you want to make a case for the Bible being fabricated by people with an agenda, you have to begin by asserting that they weren't very bright.

RELIABLE STORIES

The reliability of the Bible is something we'll never settle to the satisfaction of many skeptics. Christians are all over the map on this. Some believe the Bible must be completely true down to the tiniest detail, while others believe the Bible is reliable in all that it teaches and professes, but it has the limitations you would find in any historical document composed by humans. You better believe that both sides of this debate get riled up over this.

Wherever you land on this, it is possible that we need to spend more time asking a different question: Is the Bible true because we can prove it textually or because it accomplishes what it promises?

Most Christians I know care more about the reality of Christ in their lives on a day-to-day basis. While the reliability of the Bible is important to them, a historically accurate book is not a substitute for the present power of God in their lives. The Bible is most useful when we believe it to be true *and* God uses it to guide us into holiness and truth.

A few years ago I volunteered as an Alpha course leader at a nearby state prison. One of the quiet men in my small group named Robert caught my attention because he paid careful attention to every lesson, and over the weeks that followed, he gradually opened up to me and the other men during our meeting time.

I saw him start out as a frightened man who was afraid to speak openly and then gradually learned to confront his fears about a relapse into drugs and alcohol. He spoke with bracing honesty about his mistakes and openly shared his fears about surviving once he got out of prison. Mind you, if you know anything about the bravado of prison culture, you would have been surprised to see just how vulnerable Robert became. No one in prison willingly speaks of his fears or admits that he could falter once released without something dramatic changing his perspective.

Over the following weeks I saw Robert transition from fear to confidence, even if his confidence was tempered with a heavy dose of humility. He didn't act like he had his act together, but he knew what kind of person he didn't want to be, and he was starting to learn to trust God with his future.

When people ask me if the Bible is true, I could certainly point them to plenty of reasons why the stories are accurate and reliable. However, I find it far more compelling that the Bible speaks of healing and new life through Jesus, and people today can find *exactly that*. We can prove the reliability of plenty of ancient books, but the unique place of the Bible is that we can live in its truth today. We too can experience peace, hope, joy, healing, wisdom, and every other good thing promised in its pages.

If someone doesn't want to believe in God, that person will always find a way to discredit the Bible. In fact, we should expect a significant amount of difficulty proving the Bible as true since the events happened so long ago. The miracle of the Bible is that God still changes lives just as he said he would.

CAN YOU MAKE THE BLIND SEE IF THEY WON'T OPEN THEIR EYES?

When Jesus healed a blind man on the Sabbath, it appeared to be a rather open-and-shut case. Everyone in Jerusalem had seen the man begging. They even knew his parents and could confirm his identity. However, when Jesus made it possible for the man to see by smearing mud on his eyes, the people of Jerusalem were slow to believe that this former beggar was now able to see. The questions they asked him in John 9:8–10 betrayed their doubts: "His neighbors and those who had formerly seen him begging asked, 'Isn't this the same man who used to sit and beg?' Some claimed that he was. Others said, 'No, he only looks like him.' But he himself insisted, 'I am the man.' 'How then were your eyes opened?' they asked."

When his neighbors couldn't settle the matter, they brought in the religious authorities. However, things didn't get better since they had their doubts about Jesus. "Some of the Pharisees said, 'This man is not from God, for he does not keep the Sabbath'" (John 9:16). Right from the start of their inquiry, the Pharisees had ruled out the possibility of Jesus being from God and healing the man. Even when the man's parents were brought in for questioning, the Pharisees let everyone know that siding with Jesus meant being kicked out of the synagogue.

As it turns out, no matter what anyone said, the Pharisees refused to believe in Jesus. Jesus couldn't be from God if he healed on the Sabbath, even if the evidence for such a miraculous sign was indisputable. They had to resort to disqualifying Jesus on a technicality.

We all have a certain bias or predisposition toward a point of view. However, the story of the blind man points us to the heart of the matter when it comes to believing in Jesus. If we don't want to believe in Jesus, we will always be able to find a loophole. Critics of the Bible will always come up with arguments to discredit the stories we read.

I will never be able to prove to anyone that the Bible is true if someone is resolved to pick it apart. The Pharisees had a well-known blind man standing in front of them who had just been healed by Jesus, and they still refused to believe. Mind you, they didn't dispute the healing. They just found a way to discredit Jesus. Such will be the case today if we try to root our faith in proving the truth of the Bible. Someone like Bart Ehrman will always poke a hole in our arguments, and if we keep arguing with the likes of him, we'll never be able to experience the healing and life promised by Jesus.

We can't provide bulletproof arguments to those determined to doubt. However, we can testify that meeting Jesus has radically reshaped our lives. We can testify that we once were blind, and now we see. A changed life is hard to disprove.

THE BIBLE AND CULTURE

LESS LOBSTER, MORE BONNETS

WHILE ATTENDING A church as a guest speaker one Sunday, a friend of mine was pulled aside by the pastor to his study before the service.

"I'm sorry," the pastor began, hardly making eye contact and red-faced. "I can't let you speak this Sunday."

That was it. He didn't offer further explanation. The pastor left my friend puzzling over the situation in his office. To his credit, my friend didn't storm out of the church. He settled into the back row for the service. When it came time for the sermon, he almost missed the pastor's invitation for him to come forward. The pastor smiled and waved to him.

This is strange, he thought.

After giving the sermon, he was once again called into the pastor's office. *What did I say to upset him now?* my friend thought.

The pastor sat down at his desk with his face in his hands. Agitated and flushed, the pastor finally found the courage to speak.

"I'm sorry. I was wrong."

My friend wasn't sure what this pastor had in mind. Wrong about what?

"I almost stopped you from speaking," the pastor continued, "because your hair is too long."

Let's step out of this office for a minute to talk about my friend's hair. That pastor may be the only person in the world who would say my friend

103

has long hair. His hair isn't short. He's not in the military. He just has normal, everyday hair. However, his hair was a little on the long side that Sunday, reaching down to the collar of his dress shirt. This *clearly* put him in the league of sinners who brashly violate Scripture, and he put his host pastor in a tight spot.

Ironically, this church of men with tightly cropped hair didn't have a single woman wearing a bonnet or head scarf in the building that Sunday. For all of their effort to be biblical about the length of my friend's hair, they overlooked a minor detail in Paul's epistle to the Corinthians. Let's see if you can spot it.

I once had an idea for a fake biblical head-covering business. I even thought about buying a domain name and creating a fake Twitter handle as an April Fool's joke. There would be different models, such as the elegant purple "Lydia" scarf, the rugged tent fabric "Priscilla" covering, and the more edgy "Rahab," a red ribbon for women with nothing to hide. Unfortunately, I had to scrap this idea since truth is stranger than fiction.

After a few seconds of online research, I found a list of "prayer" covering websites:

Headcoverings by Devorah, www.headcoverings-by
-Devora.com
Covered4Him, www.covered4him.com
Garlands of Grace, www.garlandsofgrace.com
ModestWorld.com, www.modestworld.com
MyHeadcoverings.com, www.myheadcoverings.com
Plain and Simple Headcoverings, www
.prayercoverings.com
Plainly Dressed, www.plainlydressed.com

I'm especially interested in the marketing plan for the sites that emphasize being "plain." Can you imagine the marketing team trying to think of ways to say, "Ours is the plainest clothing on the entire Internet"?

Judge for yourselves: Is it proper for a woman to pray to God with her head uncovered? Does not the very nature of things teach you that if a man has long hair, it is a disgrace to him, but that if a woman has long hair, it is her glory? For long hair is given to her as a covering. If anyone wants to be contentious about this, we have no other practice—nor do the churches of God. (1 Cor. 11:13-16)

Besides mandating long hair for women, Paul made it *very* clear that he wasn't in the mood to debate the necessity of women covering their heads when praying. It was the only way to do it.

Before we sit back and have a laugh at this church and their hairy rules, let's not forget that every church does something like this. We all set up certain rules without realizing potential conflicts and contradictions within Scripture based on cultural assumptions. Oftentimes the most destructive aspects of Christianity for those growing up in the church are tied to a failure of Christians to discern which aspects of the Bible are linked to another cultural time and place. A few of the trends I've observed include:

Women are discouraged from pursuing careers that may in fact be a God-given calling.

Men are pressured to avoid all career uncertainty in order to provide for their families.

Children are disciplined in painful and crushing ways.

Young men are trained in an authoritative, almost military template for manhood.

Young women are encouraged to marry and to submit their desires to their husbands.

Single men and women feel incomplete before God.

Women in verbally or physically abusive marriages have been told they should stay in order to win over their husbands rather than rescuing themselves and possibly their children.

Church leaders use the Bible to control and manipulate members.

Church members use the Bible to control and manipulate their leaders.

ABUSING THE BIBLE AND AUTHORITY IN THE HOME?

Some of the most contentious conversations in Christian circles these days revolve around what a "biblical family" looks like. There are groups who support large families, others who emphasize the authority of fathers, and still others who emphasize the importance of using physical discipline for children, even at the extremely young age of one. While there are many well-meaning and good people involved in these groups, there are many well-documented cases of emotional and physical abuse, as well as extreme cases of manipulation and financial control. At the heart of these groups are Bible verses about disciplining children, gender roles, and the relationship between husbands and wives. These verses can be used to justify abuse, control, and manipulation.

My pastor once shared a helpful test to determine whether someone is misusing the Bible to justify abuse: "Jesus never hurts or abuses you. If someone is using Jesus to hurt or abuse you, that person is misusing the Bible." Homes will look different as we try to apply the Bible's ancient family structures to our modern world in a variety of ways, and the central issue is whether husbands or parents misuse the Bible to justify destructive behavior. Need more information? Here are some resources to consider from the perspective of recovering survivors:

Quivering Daughters, www.quiveringdaughters.com
Recovering Grace, www.recoveringgrace.org
No Longer Quivering, www.patheos.com/blogs/
    nolongerquivering/
Christians for Biblical Equality, www.cbeinternational
    .org, especially the magazine issue "The Sons
    and Daughters of the Christian Patriarchy
    Movement," *Mutuality* 19, no. 1 (Spring
    2012), http://www.equalitydepot.com/
    patriarchymovementinchristianity.aspx
Good Women Project, www.goodwomenproject.com
Toxic Faith by Stephen Arterburn and Jack Felton[1]
The Subtle Power of Spiritual Abuse by David Johnson and
    Jeffrey VanVonderen[2]

These may strike some as extreme examples, but as I meet Christians, I often hear stories about ways a misunderstanding about the Bible's original setting led to Christian movements that left a lot of wounds and scars. Today you can find blogs and websites full of survivors of these movements.

We talk about biblical marriage, but there were many aspects of "biblical" marriages that we would never consider for a modern marriage today, such as a young man marrying the widow of his brother, a victorious Israelite army "marrying" female captives, or a man taking multiple wives—why hello there David, the man after God's own heart.

We talk about biblical preaching, but every sermon recorded in the New Testament is quite short. In light of this, did God intend for sermons to be short? Keep in mind that the one time we hear about Paul preaching into the night, *someone died*. I, for one, would far prefer that churches work on getting this biblical preaching business set straight.

We talk about biblical manhood or biblical womanhood, but can we really compare modern, industrial, and digital society to an agrarian world where most every family worked from home, scratching out an existence together? When it comes to "biblical" families and gender roles, can an ancient, patriarchal culture where women had no rights offer up specific and definitive guidelines for us today?

We could talk about a biblical approach to government, but then the ancient world generally linked government and religion. The Romans had even gone so far as deifying Caesar. That made life quite convenient for Roman rulers, but "honoring" the government was a tricky matter for Christians in New Testament times.

All of this relates to the thorny issue of the Bible and culture. While we can all agree that God reveals himself in a particular time and place, even my use of the male pronoun in this sentence hints at the limits we face when describing God with our finite languages, categories, and experiences. In other words, the appearance of God in a particular culture does not necessarily consecrate that culture's standards and practices as the norm for all time.

For some, this is an obvious challenge that comes up when reading an ancient book in the modern world. For others, the thought of leaving behind the mindset "God said it, I believe it, and that settles it" can feel like jumping into an abyss. And then there are those who grew up in churches that didn't acknowledge the complexity of the Bible and culture and suffered greatly for one of the reasons listed above.

The connection between the Bible and culture determines some extremely important decisions that include where we go to church, what career we choose or don't choose, how we raise our children, how we live day to day in our homes, and whether we feel liberated or oppressed by the Bible. For many white men like myself, this hasn't been quite as urgent an issue. However, for many women and racial minorities in America, this is a defining issue that can alter the course of their lives and define their relationship with Christianity.

Before we look at the complexities at play here, we need to revisit a question we were pondering earlier but now look at from a different perspective: Why do we read the Bible?

WHY DO WE READ THE BIBLE?

Do we read the Bible to find the answers and rules?

Do we read the Bible to find God?

These two questions could lead to a false dichotomy for some. Don't we need to live holy lives that follow the rules in order to know God? There's an element of truth here, but the issue is that we read the Bible in order to know God, and then the promised Holy Spirit guides us into all truth. While we use the Bible for guidance and even memorize Scripture, we aren't necessarily picking up a script we're supposed to follow word for word in every situation. In fact, following the Bible as a script, word for word, could be used to undermine what the Bible stands for—a possibility that the Bible itself suggests.

As Jesus and his disciples walked through the fields at harvest time, they started to pick heads of grain. We don't know the exact details of this situation, but it's quite likely that they needed a meal and were gleaning heads of grain. This wasn't a light snack just because they wanted to kill some time.

However, they were gleaning these heads of grain on the Sabbath. The Jewish leaders who had become experts at following the law with precision and had developed their own oral traditions to ensure they obeyed the law perfectly didn't hesitate to challenge Jesus. Jesus' disciples were clearly working on the Sabbath.

Jesus could have debated them on the grounds that picking grain wasn't "work" per se. However, he didn't debate them on that point. He struck right at the heart of their interpretive system. Jesus argued that working on the Sabbath was permissible, especially in the case of showing mercy to those in need. His disciples needed food, and therefore they received a free pass for "working" on the Sabbath. In fact, Jesus even stressed that he's not the first person to "break" the Sabbath in such a way. David himself did the same thing when he took consecrated bread to feed his men. Jesus also used similar reasoning when he healed a man with a deformed hand, arguing that the Sabbath is a day for doing good and showing mercy, even if that requires "doing work."

I can't emphasize enough what Jesus did: he broke down literal systems of interpreting the Bible by pointing to God's higher ethics of mercy and love. Jesus used the example of David breaking the Sabbath to feed his men, and let's not overlook this point: Jesus didn't defend himself by arguing over the particulars of breaking the Sabbath. He didn't look for loopholes or lines of reasoning to beat the teachers of the law at their own game. He told them that they were playing the wrong game with the Scriptures.

They had missed the focus on mercy and love throughout the Scriptures.

When I finally saw the radical nature of Jesus' message, I realized that he would ruffle quite a few feathers today as well—including my own! We want clear rules to follow and standards to uphold, but Jesus told his original audience that these standards weren't as useful as learning to act in love, justice, and mercy. Even if his critics had devised ways to "obey" the Bible perfectly, they had missed the point.

Am I the only person who finds that challenging?

HOLD THE LOBSTER

Cultural issues can be some of the most troublesome interpretive issues for certain Christians and would-be Christians today. Can women teach in church? What has the church's role been in promoting slavery? How does the Bible speak to issues of race and reconciliation? Does homosexuality even qualify as a cultural issue in Scripture?

We have no problem today sorting out certain cultural aspects of the Bible. We can set aside the Jewish dietary laws that prohibit lobster, shellfish, and other restrictions because the Spirit told the early church to remove them from the Christian life. We have also finally figured out that slavery is, in fact, quite wrong. It took us a couple thousand years and the Civil War in America to make up our mind on that one since the proponents of slavery supposedly had a plain, literal reading of the Bible on their side.

LIBERATING A STORY

What is the exodus story about?
    Is it about slaves being liberated by God?
    Is it about a chosen people conquering the Promised Land?
    We would most likely argue that both are true. However, in the history of America these two story lines from the narrative in the book of Exodus were adopted by two very different groups.
    The European settlers of America believed that America was the new Promised Land for a new people of Israel. To a certain degree, these early Americans were right to have felt that way since many of them were religious refugees, escaping to the relative freedom of America. However, the biblical text doesn't exactly encourage reinterpreting the Promised Land for a new nation, and this remixing of the exodus story soon led to injustice and exploitation. In fact, as many Americans, in both the North and the South, used slave labor and the slave trade to build their wealth, we could argue that America became a land of broken promises for many people.
    Speaking of the people enslaved in the new Promised Land, they also clung to the exodus story. However, instead of seeing America as a new Promised Land filled with opportunity, they saw America as Egypt and identified themselves with the plight of the enslaved Israelites. For them, the story of Israelite exodus from Egypt spoke to their struggles as slaves who hoped and prayed that God would send a Moses to free them.
    What is the exodus story really about? It depends who you ask.

It's far more difficult to sort out what to make of the Bible's commands for families, morality, churches, businesses, and government. Did the writers of the Bible really intend to set up a systematic, internally consistent guide for all of life over the course of thousands of years? Or did they pray to God in the midst of their daily lives, growing up, marrying, worrying about foreign invaders, harvesting their crops, praying, celebrating with neighbors, mourning over tragedy, and seeking God's direction for their lives? How did the writers of Scripture intend future generations to read the events, prayers, and prophecies they recorded?

We already know how to study the Bible in its original context. However, applying the Bible to our lives today is far more difficult. We don't just study the Bible in its original context and then arrive at a clear conclusion every single time. While we can sometimes find a clear application, such as worship no other God than the Lord, there are other topics that are far more difficult to discern. For instance, most Christians generally understand that the Bible doesn't speak to every possible situation where divorce may be necessary, especially situations with physical or verbal abuse.

Adding to the mix of complexity are the traditions of the church passed down to us, traditions that were developed in their own setting with their own values and norms. It's not surprising that the historic church was generally opposed to women teaching or stressed male headship in the home[3] since the entire culture revolved around male leadership and patriarchal family structures where only the men could inherit property, vote, and, for the most part, run a business. Adding to the mix of the Bible's setting and the traditions passed down to us that shape what we believe, we have our own values and expectations that define the way we read the Bible as well.

How do we discern what is "right" if we're trying to balance the influence of the values of the Bible's culture, the values of historic Christians, and our values today?

How do we "distill" a key lesson from Bible stories that took place thousands of years ago?

There are two extremes that we want to avoid here. We don't want to assume that our values today are superior to those found in the Bible and that our personal preferences always win when stacked up against the

Bible. However, we also don't want to impose all of the values from the times of the Bible into the present, let alone the future. While the stories in Scripture consistently show that God was far more just and progressive than most cultures that existed alongside the Israelites, we still wouldn't take Israel's "progressive" laws governing the treatment of slaves in the ancient world and apply them to our culture today.

The stakes here are incredibly high. We don't want to say that the Bible has no meaning or that it could mean almost anything. However, there is no Christian today who applies everything from the Bible literally. Whether we go easy on head coverings and hair length or we all make decisions about what to apply and what to ignore, the big difference is our awareness of what we're doing. Can we ensure that we don't threaten our own faith or the faith of others with the way we apply the Bible?

FOR IMMEDIATE RELEASE
NEW FROM EPHESUS PRESS: *THE PAPYRUS DRIVEN CHURCH* BY PAUL THE APOSTLE

In this definitive "how to" book for church planters and missionaries, the apostle Paul shares the secrets he learned after planting churches throughout the Roman Empire that determine for all time the most effective ways to plant and lead churches. Paul shares how to avoid getting shipwrecked by a nor'easter, how to survive a shipwreck if the captain won't listen, how to pay your own way through tentmaking, how to pastor churches through letter writing, how to multitask while chained to a soldier, and tips for avoiding angry, rock-throwing mobs.

In this deeply practical and instructive book, Paul provides the final answers to the most pressing questions in the church today, including qualifications for pastors, circumcision guidelines, household roles, marriage instructions for widows, and effective insults for false teachers. The final chapter provides an advanced series of teachings on how to pray in tongues, how to visit heaven in a vision, and how to hand sinners over to Satan.

THE CULTURALLY PURE BIBLE

I've heard more than a few Christians say something like the following:

> "I wish we could get back to the simplicity of the New Testament!"
> "I'm just a follower of Jesus. I don't get involved in religion."
> "If we could only get past our assumptions, we'll be able to really find the truth in the Bible."

There's an assumption that following Jesus used to be simple and pure at one point, and that if we just studied the New Testament extra carefully, we'd arrive at a pure perspective that is completely free from any kind of cultural bias. Yet that perspective simply isn't possible for us. And that is both good and challenging.

For starters, we need to stop thinking of different cultures and values as enemies. Each culture is a context that God spoke into, whether that's the original time of the Bible, the historic church that shaped what we believe, or our own culture today. Some are more problematic or troubling than others, but I'm grateful that the writers of the Bible were inspired to speak God's words into a particular time and place. God is willing to meet his people where they're at.

That leaves us with a challenging situation when it comes to interpreting the Bible today, but all is not lost.

SPIRITUALLY GUIDED, COMMUNITY-CENTERED BIBLE READING

We should rightly be concerned that this discussion of the Bible and culture could open too many possibilities for reshaping the Bible according to an individual's personal taste or permit a particular time period from the past to determine how we always interpret the Bible. I don't think we have a clear blueprint for how to always arrive at the right conclusion for the study of Scripture. There will always be some tensions. I don't expect Christians to agree on how to interpret passages related to sensitive topics like women in ministry, gender roles in a marriage, or the especially divisive issue of LGBT practice.

We want to let God have authority in our lives. Therefore we use the Bible as our source of guidance for church, daily choices, and spiritual living. However, no one is consistently "biblical" because everything in the Bible needs to be interpreted for us today. Some passages are easier than others, but no one is able to follow the Bible like a blueprint. Otherwise, women would be wearing bonnets to church and men would need to keep their hair short.

All is not lost.

Jesus promised that the Holy Spirit would lead his followers into the truth. Paul backed him up on this as well. In addition, the Holy Spirit has been given to every follower of Jesus, and so we can interpret the Bible in community and run our interpretations by one another. This happened in Acts when Peter had a vision that God had declared all food clean and then later when Paul and Barnabas argued that circumcision and the law of Moses were no longer necessary for Greek converts to Christianity. Can we imagine anyone proposing today that—*gasp*—parts of the Bible no longer applied? That's exactly what the Holy Spirit did. And while I'm not suggesting that we should start chopping away the verses of the Bible that we dislike, the Holy Spirit will guide us toward how to apply the truths of Scripture.

For instance, if a wife leaves her husband, the first reaction of some "biblical" Christians may be to condemn her. The husband may even take his case to the church elders. However, instead of treating this woman as an unbeliever, the Spirit may guide the church to compassionately examine the wife's perspective. Was the husband verbally abusive? Was the husband cruel to their children? The Spirit provides guidance for us today when love and compassion are necessary. Keep in mind that when presented with a perfectly lawful opportunity to stone a woman caught in adultery, Jesus chose mercy instead of the law's mandated punishment of death (Lev. 20:10). We can't question Jesus' commitment to the Bible, and so we have to acknowledge that there's something else going on with Scripture beyond providing the biblical blueprint for living.

We read the Bible in communion with the Holy Spirit and our communities so that we can draw near to God and be transformed. We're not looking for loopholes. We're hoping that God will write his laws on our hearts (Jer. 31:33; Heb. 10:16) rather than on handmade bindings across our foreheads.

The guidance of the Holy Spirit and the Christian community isn't as neat and tidy as simply "taking the Bible literally." Left to our own devices we may confuse an older culture's standards with God's perspective or we may read the Bible selectively, permitting our current values to always

HOW TO WIN A BIBLE INTERPRETATION ARGUMENT

Tired of fellow Christians messing with your theology? Want a surefire way to win a Bible argument? Here's a 100 percent reliable way to win an argument over interpreting the Bible every single time:

Suggest that your opponent doesn't love the Bible, respect the Bible, or believe in the truthfulness of the Bible. No need for empathy or listening. Just cast your opponent out of the church and demand repentance.

You can take things a step further by saying that your opponent is allowing their sinful depravity to cloud their reading of the Bible. By truly remaining open to the direction of God, the other person will come around to your perspective.

Want to go nuclear? Suggest that your opponent hates the Bible and is deceived by Satan himself. That will effectively derail any meaningful conversation away from the interpretive issue at hand and redirect the conversation to the spiritual status of your opponent.

trump the guidance of Scripture. In the end, we may end up only misleading ourselves or hurting someone else. However, the community of believers teamed up with the Holy Spirit provides a far safer way to go. As we learn to listen to the voice of the Spirit and submit our readings of Scripture to one another, we'll be challenged to rethink our interpretations and will place ourselves in a far better position to spot the challenges of the Bible and culture.

It's not a free-for-all if we acknowledge the influence of culture on the Bible. Seeing the influence of culture gives us clarity about our limitations and creates more awareness for dialogue with our traditions and other Christians so we can catch our oversights and focus on Christ at the center of Christianity.

Perhaps we need a new motto: "God spoke through my Bible-immersed, Spirit-led community, I am in dialogue with it, that settles it . . . until our next conversation." I may need to work on the wording for that.

NO DOUBT?

ARE CHRISTIANS BEYOND A DOUBT?

I USED TO THINK THAT doubting God or the Bible was the trendy thing to do. I probably saw it in a light similar to teenage rebellion.

"Oh, look at you, all grown up like and questioning things. Well aren't you *original*? You know who else doubts God? *Satan!*"

Then I had doubts of my own. Suddenly I wasn't able to swat away my own nagging questions and troubling experiences. I also realized that I needed to respond to those who doubted with more compassion and understanding.

I have several friends who continue to practice as Christians, but they don't know what to think about God. They are essentially "Christian agnostics." For far too long I just wanted to stick a band-aid on their wounded faith. I wanted to make things better, and I wanted that to happen *now*. It's jarring to learn that the answers and experiences that worked for me didn't do it for them.

I could tell them about some of my most formative and dramatic prayer experiences, and they may just shrug.

I could tell them about the people who have made enormous sacrifices for others in the name of Christ, and they nod in appreciation that some Christians are committed to living like Jesus.

It's also easy for Christians to be dismissive toward those who have

> "Faith is a way of waiting—never quite knowing, never quite hearing or seeing, because in the darkness we are all but a little lost. There is doubt hard on the heels of every belief, fear hard on the heels of every hope, and many holy things lie in ruins because the world has ruined them and we have ruined them. But faith waits even so, delivered at least from that final despair which gives up waiting altogether because it sees nothing left worth waiting for."
>
> —Frederick Buechner, *Secrets in the Dark*[1]

doubts about the faith because we really, really don't want to have the same problems. It's disturbing to hear that someone who grew up in the same church as you and attended all of the same Bible studies and prayed all of the same prayers is either doubting God or thinking of leaving the faith altogether. Let's be honest about the problem here: if this person is about to leave the faith or has already left the faith, why can't the same thing happen to you as well?

We fear that doubt is contagious, especially if someone has had experiences similar to our own. Doubt can be especially difficult for pastors who feel isolated and responsible for the health of their congregations. For starters, admitting doubt is a fast track to losing your job and all security for your family. The job market isn't exactly exploding with positions for pastors who don't believe in God. In addition, if a pastor shares doubts from the pulpit, there is a fear that members of the congregation who haven't struggled with Christianity could be introduced to new issues with the faith.

There aren't very many incentives for pastors to address doubts, whether their own or the doubts of others, and there are plenty of reasons why Christians are hesitant to speak with a friend or neighbor about their doubts. On the other side of this discussion, I know that many of us fear offering trite solutions to a friend's doubts. At least, I fear doing that now after making some pretty insensitive mistakes.

What should we do about doubts?

We don't want doubts to linger, but we need to address them patiently and honestly. Where do we begin?

THE ABRIDGED, DOUBT-FREE BIBLE

If every person who doubted God was removed from the Bible, it would be a very short book. Doubt is often presented as a horrible problem that brings about dire consequences, and there certainly are plenty of stories where doubt led to suffering and heartbreak. Jesus told his followers that they should pray with confidence and James wrote that those who doubt are double-minded and will not receive anything they ask for from God.

We get the impression that a little bit of doubt can ruin everything. *A lot* of doubt is a sure recipe for disaster.

There certainly may be times when doubt can prove extremely problematic for a Christian, but let's take a look at a few key Bible stories to see what God did when his people struggled with doubt.

When God called Moses, Moses couldn't stop thinking of the reasons why he was the wrong guy. He stuttered and wasn't good at making speeches. Even when God recruited his brother to do all of the heavy lifting in front of Pharaoh, Moses still begged God to send someone else. That wasn't exactly a vote of confidence for the one true God. Of course we all know how that story worked out.

While I'm not usually a big fan of the book of Judges, let's look at a judge that God chose to lead Israel: Gideon. He really didn't want to fight the Midianites. How could God beat such a powerful armed force with "warrior camels"—the tanks of the ancient world? The horseless and camel-less Israelites would get trampled for sure. But God promised Gideon the victory. This promise wasn't good enough, and so Gideon "fleeced" God—twice. While we may imagine God sending a thunderbolt down to smite Gideon, he played along, soaking and un-soaking the fleece until Gideon ran out of ideas for his fleece.

When the entire nation of Israel turned away from God, God still reached out to them through the prophet Elijah. Elijah confronted the prophets of Baal on Mount Carmel while the people stood back watching. We don't read about the people doing anything beyond toe-tapping spectating. They weren't willing to offer their allegiance to either side unless something happened. We usually think that faith must precede every act of God, but sometimes God surprised the Israelites with an extraordinary act to win them back.

Moving on to the disciples of Jesus in the New Testament, let's just say that Jesus wouldn't have had a single disciple if doubt disqualified anyone from following him. While the women who followed Jesus had a relatively reliable track record, persevering through some of Jesus' darkest hours, the disciples he chose were all over the place. We give Thomas a hard time as a doubter, but let's face it: those guys were all a mess. At times Jesus' catchphrase became, "Why do you have so little faith?" (Matt. 6:30; 8:26; 14:31; 16:8; 17:20). They didn't know he was the Messiah for quite some time, and even when they started to believe it, Jesus ended up being a completely different Messiah than the one they'd hoped for. When faced with potentially losing their lives alongside Jesus, they all ran for it. Didn't they have faith in Jesus?

Is doubt a good thing? Well, it's certainly not God's ideal. However, the consistent theme throughout Scripture is that God can work with people in the midst of their doubts. Doubt is not a deal breaker. God is patient and powerful enough to wait out our doubts and to win us back, although we should be wary of holding on to our doubts instead of the promises of God. The key to survival has to do with the math of doubt.

THE MATH OF DOUBT

If you're struggling with doubt, then you're in a place where your belief and unbelief are held in conflict with each other. It's not a comfy place to be, but Jesus can work with it. While we are warned against "doubting" Jesus, doubt does not disqualify us right from the start. There's still quite a lot we can do.

We tend to think that a little bit of doubt can erase a lot of faith. Is a little bit of faith wiped out by a lot of doubt? All of that doubt must be stronger, right?

That's not how the math of faith and doubt works.

When a man brought his demon-possessed son to be healed by Jesus' disciples, he had to endure the agony of watching these holy men fail over and over again. Let's remember that casting out demons was a thing back then. There were others who could cast out demons as well. Jesus' disciples saw them as competitors in fact. For some reason this demon wouldn't budge.

By the time this father brought his son to the disciples, his faith was certainly wavering. Everyone had failed him. Perhaps Jesus was his last shot before giving up. His doubt and frustration came through loud and clear to Jesus. When Jesus rebuked him and told him to have faith, the father said one of the most honest things ever in the history of humanity, "I believe; help my unbelief."

He knew that he was struggling with doubt, but some part of him still believed. He had brought his son to Jesus after all, so he wasn't completely lost in apathy or despair. He had a tiny bit of faith left, even though he felt overwhelmed by unbelief. You could say this little faith was like a mustard seed. Jesus said that faith like this can move a mountain, most likely meaning it could accomplish more than the military might of Rome (a reference to the "mountain" of rocks and earth that were moved in order to build Herod's fortress called the Herodium). It's comforting to see how Jesus honored the father's small, faltering faith.

I used to think that the mere mention of doubt was the end of prayer time. Who could "believe" in Jesus or ask Jesus to do anything while still harboring doubts? That guy! Jesus healed his son even though he confessed doubts.

The math of faith and doubt goes like this:

A little faith > a lot of doubt.

Doubt does not necessarily cancel faith. There may be times when doubt will hold us back from God, but there is a process and a tension to faith and doubt.

What would James say about this?

James wasn't a big fan of doubt. He wrote this about prayer: "But when you ask, you must believe and not doubt, because the one who doubts is like a wave of the sea, blown and tossed by the wind. That person should not expect to receive anything from the Lord. Such a person is double-minded and unstable in all they do" (James 1:6-8).

Perhaps this is too fine a line, but there is a huge difference for me between someone who is completely convinced that God doesn't exist and the person who prays and confesses struggles with unbelief. The mere mention of our doubts to God shows that we are at least stable enough to think there's a chance God can do something about them. Sometimes the most faith-filled thing you can do is to tell God about all of your doubts, even if you aren't sure what's going to happen next.

What if we let God become a part of the process of our believing?

What would happen if we spoke completely honestly to God about everything we don't understand or struggle to believe?

Doesn't it take faith to just admit such things in the first place?

It's not like faith is a commodity that someone can buy and own— something that you either have or don't have. Faith isn't instant all of the time. Faith is often a process. Perhaps we overemphasize dramatic conversion stories to the detriment of those who have struggled for their hard-won faith over a series of conversations or after years of struggling with Scripture. Then again, faith is something that can wilt and struggle. Having faith once is not a guarantee of its continued survival.

DON'T LET DOUBT GROW

I call it the demon weed. It's a thick weed that runs deep into our garden before sending out enormous leaves that will shade a huge section of our raised beds if I let it grow. In fact, the longer I let it grow, the more costly it will be to remove it. The first summer it popped up, I didn't notice it right away, and we lost a section of Swiss chard all around the weed after I dug it out. Every time I see the demon weed begin to rise, it's like a call to arms as I rush to the garage for my extra sharp spade and begin digging away.

Weeds are inevitable in a garden. You can't grow anything worth eating without a little competition from weeds—even demon weeds. However, the presence and persistence of weeds does not mean we should just give in to them. Like weeds, doubt may stay with us longer than we would like, and sometimes it doesn't come out on our own timetable. Sometimes we'll be stuck with doubts that persist for years even as we struggle to have faith. That is the challenge we face each day: reaching out for God even if we are wrestling with doubts.

REASONS TO STOP BELIEVING

There are many reasons why someone may stop believing in God. Some find the concept of God hard to understand and accept. Others struggle to believe in the Bible. Still others are turned off by all organized religion and don't see a need for God. Sometimes "evidence" for God isn't convincing for an atheist. If you want to learn more about what atheists are thinking, my friend Alise hosted a blog series dedicated to dialogue with atheists titled "A Christian Guide to Atheists," www.alise-write .com/category/the-christian-guide-to-atheists/.

Without faith, it is impossible to please God, let alone to find God in the first place. Finding God means we have to take a leap into the unknown, stepping into a place that may feel uncertain. I don't want to minimize the importance of taking that first step toward believing in God, risking that God can be present for us. We can't wallow in our doubts forever without consequence. Our doubts are not our friends.

However, without honesty, it's impossible for God to heal us.

Doubts will come. We can't avoid them. The best that we can do is to acknowledge them before God and people we trust, committing to the long-term process of sorting things out the best we can. A little bit of faith in the midst of big doubts will be enough to hold on, but our doubts are not the kinds of things that we should nurture.

Doubts can be a bit like weeds that will crowd out the life of God in us if allowed to grow unchecked.

I used to think of the parable of the sower as a statement about a future set in stone: which kind of soil are you? I've since come to think of this parable as more of a lesson in spiritual growth and the danger of neglect (Luke 8:4–15).

Anyone who has gardened knows that you make soil fertile by cultivating it with compost, manure, and organic matter like leaves. Only a lazy gardener fails to pull out the rocks from his soil and lets weeds and brambles take hold. What if the parable about the sower is about the kind of environment we cultivate for the Word of God in our lives? In other words, faith takes preparation. We need to make room in our lives for faith and deal with our doubts as they spring up.

Faith isn't something we've been given for all time. It is a gift we've been given and we cannot do anything to earn it, but we will lose our grip on this gift from God if we don't create room for the life of God each day. We can't always stop doubt from sprouting in our lives, but we can control the daily practices that create space for the gospel to take root and grow in our lives. Even the way the kingdom of God spreads is a mystery that seemingly happens overnight. We won't find answers to all of our questions. In fact, we may only find more questions for a time. However, as we let the gospel take root in our lives, it can grow more powerful than our doubts and give us the confidence we need to face them without fear.

SURVIVING DOUBT

My darkest days as a follower of Jesus came when I felt like prayer wasn't working. I felt like I was just talking to myself in an empty room. Quieting myself to "hear" God really didn't work. In fact, that just made things worse. The longer I waited with nothing happening, the more my anxiety kicked into gear, worrying that God really wasn't going to respond.

I know that some Christians go through a season of doubt like this and can't survive. They can't find God and choose to give up. In my own case, I held on. I can't make it sound like I did something better, but I just know that I ended up in a different place. The more I talked to trusted friends and family members, the more they prayed for me and helped me deal with my anxiety and feelings of unworthiness before God.

I had to make some uncomfortable confessions during those years of uncertainty. However, God showed up in some significant ways as friends and family prayed for me. Oftentimes they offered to pray for me, knowing exactly what I needed before I even asked for anything.

In retrospect, I see myself hanging on to God by my fingertips and a number of people pulling me back up to my feet inch by inch. The more isolated I became from other Christians, the harder it became to deal with my doubts. The more I opened myself up to people I trusted, the more steps I could take toward faith and hope.

A "DOUBT" SURVIVAL TIP

Doubt will never be more powerful in your life than when you face it alone. Doubt and loneliness can destroy your faith because you'll become convinced that there's no way forward. The only way I've seen Christians survive doubt is by processing their struggles within a safe, supportive Christian community. In fact, when you talk about your doubts with trusted friends, you'll most likely find people who have experienced similar struggles who can empathize with you and pray for you.

That's a hard thing for me to say here. Most of us fear what our friends, small group leaders, and pastors will think of us if we say what we really think. However, the Christian faith spread and grew in the first place because people talked to each other. The word "witness" occurs over and over again in the book of Acts because the message of Jesus spread through stories and personal testimonies. As followers of Jesus shared their personal stories about meeting with Jesus, they were able to invite their listeners to become disciples as well. Faith often comes through hearing.

As much as we need people who can hear our honest questions and doubts when we're in a hard spot, we also need to hear the stories of Jesus and learn from the faith of others. Having said that, there are those who aren't willing to empathize with us or honor our struggles. Those aren't the kinds of people we should seek out! We need people who can sit with us in the tension between our experiences and their own.

My current pastor has seen so many people come to faith in Jesus because he gave them space to process their beliefs. He welcomes them where they're at, pointing out the common ground between them and Jesus and then welcoming them to look into the details further. Perhaps we've overemphasized the importance of making sure everyone is on the exact same page or has prayed the same prayer. We all find God through different questions and processes. The end result is that Jesus saves. The catch is that sometimes faith comes in an instant, sometimes it takes years, and sometimes it's lost and only found many years later.

As seriously as we need to take doubt as a long-term threat if it's allowed to grow and overshadow the voice of God in our lives, doubt also simply comes with the territory if you're living by faith. Doubt is the dark side of the coin for Christianity. We won't have 100 percent perfect faith all of the time.

Have you ever worried about God's provision or doubted God?

You're in good company.

Every person who followed Jesus in the New Testament passed through a time of doubt and even struggled with doubts after discovering that Jesus truly was the Messiah. If you haven't ever doubted something about God, you will eventually. It's a good thing we know that God answers prayers that confess, "Help my unbelief." The tiny seed of faith in that prayer is more than enough to help us survive when doubts threaten to upend our faith.

APOCALYPSE NOW?

YAY! IT'S THE END OF THE WORLD!

DURING MY TEEN years we started listening to a Christian radio station that played a pastor's sermons every morning. He was preaching through the entire Bible, and that meant I began to dread the inevitable conclusion of his series in the book of Revelation. Revelation left me terrified of one-world governments imprisoning Christians, plagues destroying people and animals, angels killing at will, and then Jesus returning to bathe his enemies in their own blood.

If there's one book that could lead a Christian away from God, it has to be Revelation. There is no book that appears to be quite so violent at face value or causes so much fear among readers. I've struggled for years with Revelation, alternating between terror at the possibility of the world being engulfed by violence and confusion over the kind of God it presented. While I liked the idea of God whisking his people up to heaven in the rapture before the tribulation, I still struggled with the possibility of God violently destroying the earth and just about everyone in it. Didn't God declare creation "good"? And so much for that rainbow God gave Noah and the animals. God deftly promised to never destroy the earth "with a flood," leaving the possibility to rain down fire, plagues, and blood on the earth. God had the loopholes covered.

However God sorted out the covenant with Noah, readers of the Bible today are often disturbed by the violence of the end times. Such stories are hard to reconcile with Jesus and have been hard for many Christians to grasp. There's a good reason why so many Christians avoid Revelation: it doesn't make any sense. We need to talk about Revelation in connection to our survival as Christians because there are very good reasons to believe that modern interpreters of the book of Revelation have dramatically misrepresented God and misconstrued how the events of the end times may play out.

Violent action from God isn't without precedent, at least on a small scale—hello, Sodom and Gomorrah. However, the global scale of violence in Revelation appears to be so dramatic that we owe it to God, the Bible, and ourselves to ask some tough questions about how we interpret this book. In some Christian circles the notion of the rapture and a violent tribulation headed up by the Antichrist is a foregone conclusion thanks to books such as *The Scofield Reference Bible*; *The Late, Great Planet Earth*; and the Left Behind series.

Some have attempted to link the "scenes" of Revelation with current events, leading to every conspiracy theorists' fantasy: a rich trove of numbers, symbols, beasts, and predictions that can be loosely associated with a wide variety of events. What's the "mark of the beast"? Perhaps it referred to the royal seal of Nero, but isn't it a bit more interesting to speculate about future bar-code tattoos or RFID (radio frequency identification) chips being stuck in our hands? And the various rulers and beasts were especially intimidating during the era of the Cold War when all eyes were focused on the Soviet Union. These "interpretations" spend more time studying news headlines than the historical context of Revelation and more often than not end up sowing fear and confusion. While there's nothing wrong with using Revelation or Bible prophecy in general as a jumping-off point for a novel (or sixteen), let's not confuse speculation with interpretation.

If we back away from our newspapers and apocalypse forecasts for a moment to examine Revelation within its historical context—you know, like every other book of the Bible—and hold the origins of some more recent interpretations under greater scrutiny, we may be surprised to learn

BOOK REVIEW FROM THE *EPHESUS EXPOSÉ*
"SOPHOMORE EFFORT FROM FISHERMAN CASTS WIDE
NET IN *REVELATION* BY JOHN OF PATMOS"

Dragons, beasts rising from the sea, and angel guides add elements of danger and mystery to the latest release from John of Patmos, even if they sometimes fall flat as familiar, pedantic tropes from Jewish apocalypticisms and the wildly speculative book of Daniel. John is clearly reacting to the stinging critiques of his previous eponymous release that used painfully simple Koine Greek and dragged overwrought symbols and signs through each scene. If his microcosm of a "gospel" was too reductive, obvious, and heavy-handed, his apocalypse veers toward the obscure and obstreperous with its grandiose literary aspirations and pantheon of religious symbols.

For all that is familiar and overused in *Revelation*, it's a coruscating and provocative read that offers a new-age twist from John's break-off Jewish sect of Nazarenes that reenacts a series of familiar, though sometimes tiring, biblical clichés such as the serpent vs. the woman and the plagues that precede the exodus. His opening epistolary warnings to a series of churches lends an air of urgency that drives home the many symbols of heavenly and earthly warfare that follow. No doubt his readers may puzzle over the identity of the Antichrist, but once again, John's failure to develop this character only serves to expose his limitations as an author. For all of his faux sophistication, John of Patmos remains hooked on his humble origins and has yet to produce a work of literature that will endure beyond its two-week release period. Fascinating though John's innovations may be, this humble laborer's work still smells fishy.

Flavius Josephus

that Revelation isn't a book about escape and destruction. It's actually a book about perseverance and restoration that is far less terrifying than we've been lead to imagine. Let's begin with a brief look at the origins of the so-called rapture before we drop some historical TNT into the Left Behind series.

WHERE DID THE RAPTURE COME FROM?

The idea of Christians zipping up to heaven out of thin air didn't just fall from heaven. It started to brew in the late 1700s and early 1800s. The rapture didn't take hold until an embattled Irish clergyman began to advocate for it in the 1830s.

John Nelson Darby, an Irish preacher and one of the founders of the Plymouth Brethren, had a lot of problems to solve. For starters, he had an extremely effective ministry among the lower classes of Ireland that won over many converts to the Church of Ireland, which William Magee, the Archbishop of Dublin, ruined by demanding that all converts swear allegiance to George IV as the rightful king of Ireland. Darby would have none of this, so he set out on a ministry of his own. However, while working as a freelance preacher, he also had a tough time making sense of the church, Israel, and the kingdom of God, namely: how would God fulfill all of the promises for Israel in the Old Testament in light of Jesus?

Darby believed that ancient Israel and the New Testament church

SHOULD WE LEAVE THE RAPTURE BEHIND?

While there's nothing heretical about believing in the rapture, there are some good reasons to hold it in doubt. First Thessalonians 4:15–17 has become the proof text for the rapture. However, if you line it up with similar verses like 1 Corinthians 15:23–27, there's a good reason to believe both of these passages speak of the resurrection of the dead. In his book *Surprised by Hope*, scholar N. T. Wright suggests that we read the Thessalonians passage as God's people rising in the air to meet the returning King to earth.

> When Paul speaks of "meeting" the Lord "in the air," the point is precisely not—as in the popular rapture theology—that the saved believers would then stay up in the air somewhere, away from earth. The point is that, having gone out to meet their returning Lord, they will escort him royally into his domain.[1]

have separate destinies, and this led him to make some pretty big assumptions about isolated passages of Scripture. God needed to get the church out of the way in order to deal with Israel at the end of time. Darby determined that 1 Thessalonians 4:17 spoke of Christians being removed from the earth before the end times so that God could fulfill his promises to Israel. This was an innovation of the futurist view of the end times that originally placed the majority of Revelation in the future with a "rapture" only happening at the return of Christ. Darby moved the rapture up to the beginning of Revelation before the great tribulation so that God could fulfill the promises made to Israel. Once Christians were safely tucked away in heaven, God could take out vengeance on his enemies and restore the nation of Israel. Darby wasn't the only pastor and student of Scripture reading Revelation like a literal forecast of the future that included the restoration of Israel, but he certainly did a lot to promote a pretribulation rapture among the Plymouth Brethren, whose influence later reached the fundamentalists in America through the Niagara Bible Conference and then from there to *The Scofield Reference Bible* in the early 1900s.

As *The Scofield Reference Bible* caught on in the United States, the notion of a pretribulation rapture took hold in America unlike any other place around the world. We should also note that current events before and after that time in the United States may have played a significant role in the spread of the pretribulation rapture, futurist view of Revelation in America. The upheaval of the Civil War that left thousands of families devastated by personal loss and large segments of the Confederacy in ashes created an atmosphere conducive for this new view of the end times to take hold. The possibility of escaping a world that is descending into chaos may have been appealing. By the end of the Great Depression, sales of *The Scofield Reference Bible* exceeded one million copies, and more than two million copies had sold by the end of the second of two horrific world wars.[2]

Along with the influence of C. I. Scofield's study Bible was one prolific Christian writer named Harry Ironside, also affiliated with the Plymouth Brethren, who made a statement that embodied the sense of prophetic anticipation many Christians were feeling at this time: "The moment the Messiah died on the cross, the prophetic clock stopped. There has not been a tick upon that clock for nineteen centuries."[3] The conclusion of World War II witnessed the dawn of the nuclear age and was followed in 1948 by the creation of a homeland for the Jews in Israel. All of this seemed to ready the prophetic clock for its next tick. By the time *The Late, Great Planet Earth* (1970) and the Left Behind series (1995–2007) came along, American Christians were already a receptive audience waiting to learn about the ways Revelation predicted the future and, most importantly, whisked them away from the great tribulation.

Although many Christian groups still reject Darby's "pretribulation rapture" take on the end times, including Catholics, Eastern Orthodox, and many Reformed churches, there's no denying the pervasive influence of the rapture and the "Left Behind" theology that turns Revelation into a kind of "chart of the ages" for predicting the future—an extremely violent future.

For all of the good that Darby did, we have very good reasons to question his views on the rapture and Revelation as a whole. Is it possible that we can rescue Revelation from the bloody mess that it has become? I believe so.

If the Lord delays his return, we'll do just that.

WHAT IS THE PURPOSE OF REVELATION?

Imagine you have a friend going through a really tough time as an overseas missionary. Government officials read all of the mail you send, local officials are taking every chance to make your friend suffer, and some of your friend's colleagues have even been killed because of their faith. Communication is hard to figure out, and even if you could, you wouldn't really know what to say. Where is God while his people are suffering? Is there any hope for the future?

Your only hope for encouraging your friend is to send a coded message.

The last thing you'd want to tell your friend is this: "Well, if you think things are terrible now, just wait until God comes to destroy everything!" That may be something you believe, but it's certainly the last thing you'd tell a group of suffering Christians in a letter.

Such was the situation confronting the apostle John as he wrote Revelation. While John himself was apparently dealing with being an exile stranded on an island in the western Aegean Sea, the risen Jesus made certain things known to him in a vision intended to be a blessing to servants of the Lord facing grave uncertainties. He wasn't trying to scare his original readers into believing in Jesus. He wasn't even necessarily trying to predict the future in great detail. He was trying to encourage them to persevere in the midst of severe suffering.

The potential weakness of the pretribulation rapture view is this: many interpreters have turned Revelation into a coded time line for the future without making sense of Revelation in its original setting. Rather than digging into the history of Asia Minor, the Roman Empire, or the theological background of John, we are tempted to immediately pull out our newspapers in order to speculate about the latest mark of the beast, the identity of the Antichrist, and the location of the valley of Megiddo.

If we start with the assumption that every symbol in Revelation can be linked to a literal event in the future, it's understandable that you'll end up with a violent catastrophe and an unimaginably high body count. However, there's another way to read Revelation that could point us to some other possibilities for the future of our world. Revelation may have been a letter encouraging believers to persevere in the midst of difficult times—a possibility that makes it all the more relevant for us today.

HOW SHOULD WE INTERPRET REVELATION?

There are plenty of different views of Revelation, and wherever you land is not a make-or-break matter of faithfulness to the gospel. Jesus rose from the dead and will return some day. We can all agree on that. My greater concern is that we don't advocate for a reading of Revelation that distorts the rest of the Bible and potentially alienates some people from God by portraying God in an excessively violent light. I have seen time and time again how an expectation of the rapture and the destruction of the world has undermined the kingdom of God theology Jesus taught. Instead of caring for God's creation, working toward justice for the poor, and embodying the message of the gospel, some evangelicals have used the escape narrative of Revelation to focus only on "saving souls." While the kingdom sends us out, the rapture could potentially turn its adherents into refugees who are just waiting for God to intervene.

The main idea that I'd like to propose here is that John most likely wrote a circular letter to a group of seven churches using the coded language of Jewish apocalyptic literature and a smattering of prophetic writing. While there are some aspects of Revelation that are clearly set in the future such as the white throne judgment and the New Jerusalem, it's most likely that Revelation was intended to pull back the curtain on what was already happening, as well as things that will continue to happen until the return of Christ. The past, present, and future are blended together in the book of Revelation.

As Christians in the seven churches of Asia Minor (in the western half of modern-day Turkey) suffered slander, the loss of property, the loss of work, and even death because of their allegiance to Christ, John wrote a pastoral letter that dealt with the many questions and struggles they faced.

YOU'VE GOT AN APOCALYPSE!

Apparently the Thessalonian church, if not all of the early church, expected the return of Jesus to be far less dramatic than the Left Behind blood bath. In fact, many Thessalonians had received a letter convincing them that Jesus had already returned. In 2 Thessalonians 2:1–2, Paul set them straight. They had been deceived.

Does anyone today expect news of the apocalypse to arrive via a forwarded e-mail?

In this sense, we should approach Revelation a lot like the letters we have from Paul, Peter, and James. We need to understand the cultural and religious context before we dare link John's symbols with future events.

Let's start with the apocalyptic nature of Revelation. The term *apocalypse* comes from a Greek word and means "revelation" or "disclosure," from which we get the word *apocalyptic*. Jewish writers began to write apocalyptic literature after the return from exile in Babylon led to hundreds of years living under brutally oppressive foreign rulers. As the Jewish people suffered, they took comfort in knowing that God was still reigning in heaven and that God would return to judge their oppressors. Most of these stories involved a heavenly journey guided by an angel, a world with a sharp battle between good and evil, and a future act of judgment and salvation when God returns.

Revelation isn't a pure apocalypse compared to similar books like *1 Enoch* penned by Jewish authors, but its relation is unmistakable. If anything, Revelation is a kind of Christian apocalyptic hybrid that also throws in some elements of the Old Testament prophetic writings that encouraged the Israelites to return to God, to persevere in hard times, and to wait on God's salvation. Much like apocalyptic writing, prophetic books spent more time revealing the spiritual realities of the present rather than purely predicting the future. That isn't to say that the prophets didn't predict the future. They surely did at times. However, that wasn't their only function, and the same goes for Revelation. We aren't reading a book that is primarily about the future. It mixes the present and the future together as it speaks to unseen spiritual realities. For instance, the battle between the dragon and the woman in Revelation is clearly depicting the battle between Satan and Christ that later spills over to the battle between Satan and the church. We could even say that it refers to the story of Israel, but however we take those symbols, this chapter in the middle of Revelation is hardly chronological or part of a clear time line. It's a symbolic vision that speaks to a variety of events, some of which happened in the past and some of which will continue to happen. The story of Christ and the perseverance of the suffering church plays out in this wide-ranging vision that reaches both backward and forward. Revelation certainly speaks to the future at certain points, but understanding how it spoke to the past will keep us from abusing the biblical text with too much speculation over the future.

Revelation tells us a whole lot more about how to live each day than about what the future holds. I know that's a jarring concept to propose among some Christian groups who have only focused on Revelation as a time line for the future. However, the bulk of the historical and literary evidence points to something quite different from what popular books about Revelation portray. While there are some wonderfully breathtaking aspects to the future, Revelation has far more to say about worshipping the God who has conquered evil even though we may spend today in the presence of our enemies.

WHAT IS THE MESSAGE OF REVELATION?

There's no doubt that God is angry in Revelation. However, we need to step back and ask, "What exactly is God angry about?"

God is angry about injustice and oppression throughout the earth. God is especially angry at the powers of evil and those aligned with evil who are killing his people. The martyrs are crying out in Revelation: "How long?" While the analogy isn't perfect, we can certainly compare Revelation to the exodus story. God's people must persevere through a time of suffering until God comes to deliver them and to judge their oppressors. The plagues in Revelation 15–16 should immediately echo back to the exodus story. Once again God is delivering his persecuted people from a powerful empire. The plagues were directed against the Egyptian oppressors in the exodus story, and it's likely that the same can be said in Revelation as God defeats the empire of "Babylon." While some interpreters have speculated that these plagues are literal, it's worth remembering that they are surrounded by imagery and symbols. John is pulling from literal events of the past to construct a symbolic picture that could have a variety of meanings.

In the case of the original audience, Babylon stood for the Roman Empire (see 1 Peter 5:13), but as we ponder what Revelation could mean today, Babylon could function as a type for any kind of oppressive empire that exploits the poor, perpetuates injustice, and thrives on violence. If John borrowed from the Jewish apocalyptic tradition, then it makes sense that Jews returning from exile saw Babylon as a representative for evil in the world, and John had no trouble linking the evil of Babylon with Rome.

John's message is something like this: Do you see evil and injustice in the world? Of course you do. God sees it, has conquered it through Christ, and will one day deliver his people and judge his enemies. The book of Revelation seeks to answer our pressing questions about persevering in the presence of evil, the tension of evil and a just God, and God's future plans for dealing with evil.

Could that mean America or some other nation today equals Babylon as some suggest? That's a great question, and it's one that John would want us to ask.

The book of Exodus and the Old Testament prophets, in part, provide a helpful interpretive guide to Revelation. The Beast, Antichrist, and

Dragon in Revelation are part of a long line of oppressive forces attacking the people of God and causing suffering throughout the earth. Rather than try to find a precise match between each character in Revelation and our world today, it may be far more helpful to consider the ways we can minister and share the healing power of the sacrificed Lamb who has conquered all. Jesus, the slaughtered Lamb, has all power and authority over the destructive forces in this world, and as such, Revelation is a call to trust in him and to testify to his present reign and future rule. The beginning of that visible rule on earth will be a final judgment that exposes and removes the forces of evil from the earth once and for all. While Revelation acknowledges the chaos of our world with the plagues and bowls spilling over, it also points us to a future when our worship of the Lamb will be the norm for everyone on earth.

I used to live in fear of the white throne judgment, worrying that God would see my secret deeds and expose them for all to see. While God does truly see our hidden motives, my perspective was hardly appropriate for someone who has no condemnation through Christ Jesus (Rom. 8:1-2). The purpose of this all-seeing white throne judgment is to render true justice to all. God sees our quiet, overlooked faithfulness, but he also sees the injustices and horrors of this world.

God has put the powers of this world on notice: he sees all and will judge each person's actions one day. While we rejoice in the grace and mercy of God that we have found through the cross, we also recognize that the lordship of Christ makes his judgment of this world inevitable. We wouldn't expect anything less from a good and just God. Evil and injustice must be brought before a holy and just judge who will render justice and eradicate evil.

Ironically, I've spent so much of my life fearing the power of evil, death, and destruction that I found in Revelation that I never thought of its message for people suffering persecution. I thought it was a book about a terrible future where the world spirals out of control and everyone suffers a thousand times more than today. It's far more likely that John adopted the conventions of Jewish apocalyptic literature—a genre that involved heavenly journeys in the midst of suffering and persecution and provided hope that God would one day overcome evil. Revelation acknowledges the suffering, violence, and injustice of our world and proposes that God is Lord of all in the midst of these terrible times but will appear in order to bring justice and restoration.

I've spent most of my Christian life trying to reconcile the plagues and beasts of Revelation with a God who wipes away every tear (Rev. 7:17; 21:4). If anything, Revelation itself caused many of my tears. How could it tell me about a God who wipes away tears?

Revelation's message is a symbolic, poetic, prophetic mystery where the Lamb of God has conquered all, but his creation still spirals out of control with the ravages of evil. While the Lamb of God gives the world time to repent, the people of God will suffer and struggle. They must persevere through worship and holy living, refusing to surrender to the powers of evil demanding their allegiance. God will one day bring restoration, and the delay of God isn't a sign that the death and resurrection of Christ have failed.

NEW CREATION THAT ISN'T BORING

I've sat through my share of snoozer Sunday school classes, but the worst had to be the one where we discussed heaven. What will heaven be like?

We went around the room speculating about what heaven would be like, each sharing ridiculous speculations of an unfathomable eternity with God, based largely on our suburban activities. Video games? Sure! Flowers? Well, yeah! Golf? Wait, what?

Yes, we discussed whether there would be golf. Someone in our Sunday school class loved, loved, loved golf. "I sure hope there will be golf in heaven. I just enjoy it so much."

I'm surprised I was able to keep my balance as I rolled my eyes.

I hate golf so much. I hoped it wouldn't be in heaven.

Of course we were all missing the point. Thankfully Revelation can set us back on course with the kind of future God envisions.

While we don't know how literal to take Revelation's description of the new heaven and the new earth, we can make a few conjectures. For starters, there won't be destruction or death. The "absence" of the ocean is more of a figurative statement. For the Jewish people and many others, the ocean was often a symbol of chaos and death that God alone could conquer (2 Sam. 22:4–6; Job 38:10–12; Ps. 89:8–10; Matt. 8:26–27). A future "without an ocean" is a future without chaos and destruction. In addition, death itself is thrown into the lake of fire. In its place is a heavenly city where God is at the center and the tree of life provides healing for the nations. In fact, besides the heavenly city, the entire earth will be dramatically re-created so that there is a new heaven and a new earth.

We could speculate all day about whether the streets are actually gold, the measurements are literal, or what John means when he speaks of nations coming into the city for healing. The point I take from all of this is that eternity with God will take place on a renewed earth where those

REVELATION SURVIVAL TIPS

· Look for ways Revelation resembles the prophetic books of the Old Testament, especially Daniel and Ezekiel.
· Look for connections to the first-century church.
· Expect Revelation to speak about some future events, but remember that it also spoke to its original audience and that Christians have adopted a variety of ways to explain it throughout history.

who have been raised to new life dwell together with God. God will be our focus, but we'll be living in community in a city. In addition, we'll have work to do. There will be some renewed version of the garden of Eden, and we'll have a priestly function of bringing healing to the nations.

When you think about Jesus' kingdom of God message, isn't that pretty much what we're supposed to be doing now? We're supposed to live with God as the center of our lives in Christian community where we reach out to the nations to bring God's healing. In fact, the whole point of Matthew 25 is that God's saved people will also adopt God's values and bring about the healing and justice that God desires in this world. If you "know" Jesus, you'll learn to love the same things as he does. Revelation gives us a sneak peek at the kind of future God imagines for our world. We can't make the new heaven and new earth happen on our own, but the kingdom of God leads us to start living in the present reality of God's rule in an imperfect world.

There's certainly nothing wrong with reading the Left Behind series or using a *Scofield Reference Bible*. If you want to believe in the rapture, have at it. However, this interpretation is not without some significant perils. The rapture could result in Christians essentially waiting for the escape pod to carry us out of this world—a world that God will one day blow up. It's far more likely that Revelation encourages us to hold on for God's justice and salvation as we commit ourselves to the Lamb who has conquered the forces of evil that rage in our world. While everything around us appears to be out of control, God is patiently waiting for people to repent and turn to him. His delayed justice and restoration isn't indifference or failure.

The future God plans isn't destructive. God's future has more restoration and peace than we could ever imagine. For years the book of Revelation made me want to run from God. One day I saw the closing of the book in a whole new light, "The Spirit and the bride say, 'Come!'" If Revelation leaves you afraid to "come" to God, then there's a good chance you're reading it wrong. God sees our pain and suffering in this world, and he's preparing a future with healing and justice. It's just what we've been hoping for.

PART 2

CHRISTIAN PRACTICES

SIN ADDICTION

THE FREEDOM OF RESTRAINT

YOU KNOW THAT GUY at work who rarely does his job. He mocks you and the other peons who slave away while he plays games on his computer and shuffles papers, somehow convincing your boss that he's a valuable asset. You get together with your colleagues while the coffee is brewing and talk about that sniveling, lazy jerk and his long, crooked nose.

Talk is too sedate a word for it. You slam him when he saunters in fifteen minutes late or mumble passive-aggressive replies when he asks you to cover for him during his sixth smoke break of the day. You make him the butt of your jokes and the target of your slander. He's the worst kind of person and you always feel better about yourself whenever you're done ripping into him.

And yet, you know deep down that a Christian shouldn't mock this man's character, lacking though it may be. And perhaps you shouldn't make fun of the way he slurps his coffee or the way he shoves his wispy black hair away from his forehead with a brush of his hand over and over and over again. No, the Christian way is to love this man rather than insulting him behind his back.

The tongue being a restless evil aside, you still think he kind of deserves it. It's just words after all. Really, you haven't done anything all that terrible. And as you hide behind justifications, you arrive at the real truth of

THE SEVEN DEADLY SINS

Since the fourth century, Christians have singled out no less than seven deadly sins. By allowing these sins to fester we are cutting ourselves off from God, hindering our spiritual growth, and threatening our survival as Christians.

Here's a list of the sins and some possible consequences:

1. **Pride**: Competing with God and neglecting the needs of others.
2. **Envy**: Discontent with self and leads to conflict with others.
3. **Gluttony**: Skewed sense of contentment and satisfaction. Finds joy in consumption.
4. **Lust**: Disconnected from reality, selfish, and prone to unhealthy relationships.
5. **Anger**: Obsessed with control and personal perspective. Unable to resolve conflict.
6. **Greed**: Discontent and controlled by desire for money and power.
7. **Sloth**: Listless, disconnected from others, unfulfilled, and depressed.

the matter. You don't want to stop slandering him. In fact, you can't stop. It's natural, easy, and feels good, as if you can undo his grievances against you by the power of your words.

But perhaps you haven't struggled with words. Perhaps your struggle is with lusting after a neighbor along your block. He or she often walks past your house in the evening, and you find yourself thinking about this person in very inappropriate ways. It may be the scent of his cologne that lingers or that titillating blouse she wears that sparks your imagination and leaves you burning.

While you're alone at home he sneaks into your thoughts with a seductive look or when you're driving home from work your heart beats a little faster at the thought of seeing her. This infatuation is both terrifying and wonderful, fulfilling some deep-seated desires that crave to be acknowledged even if they seem endless in their demands. You can't help but give in to them because you're not really hurting anyone, and worse than that, you don't feel like you can stop. The urges are too strong, your will too weak, and those exciting moments of surrender to lust are too exciting. In either scenario, sin has taken hold and become a master of sorts. It isn't that slander and lust are harmless sources of fun and fulfillment that God doesn't want you to have. It's that you're actually enslaved to them, letting them control you, shaping you into a different sort of person, and keeping you from the good things God has planned for you. When sin becomes an irresistible force that we cannot fight, we have a tremendous problem that must be addressed without delay.

AN INFORMATION PROBLEM

Sin can be credited in part, but not as a whole, to an information problem. If sinless perfection rested on knowing the right stuff, then we could all get seminary degrees and be set. Having passed through seminary myself and knowing many others who have, I can assure you that seminary is not the silver bullet required for dealing with let alone defeating sin. However, we do well to orient ourselves with the facts of our situation.

God is not a killjoy handing down a list of restricted activities like some kind of micromanaging boss who wants nothing more than to control the minutiae of our lives. He's not sitting up in heaven laughing at those silly Christians who are missing out on all of the fun to be had with unrestrained sexual exploits, excessive drinking, and raging anger. Christians may be a bit naïve and silly at times, perhaps we're even suckers on occasion, but we're not suckers because we miss out on the benefits of catching venereal disease, racking up a DUI, or punching through Sheetrock.

God declared creation good and then part of his creation became greedy and obsessed with its own glory. Our ancestors allowed their evil desires to rule them and these desires took shape as sin. We have followed in their footsteps ever since. The book of James says that we are tempted by evil desires, we give in to them, and then we sin.

The metaphors have changed over time—an invasion, a virus, a rebellion—but the core information we need remains the same. God is calling

SIN SURVIVAL CHECKLIST

As we confront sin in our lives, there are some basic questions that will help us take steps forward:

- Is this a sin?
- What are the consequences of this sin?
- Do I want to stop?
- Do I know how to stop?

out to us with loving overtures so that we'll become willing partners and allow him to gradually infect us with his goodness. Over time his goodness will seep out of us and into the world.

God has not made his world to be ruled by evil desires, openly indulging in the destructive, self-serving powers of sin. Seeing things for what they are, we are beings shaped in the divine image of God who were made to live in loving relationship with our Creator and our fellow human beings. When we resist this calling, we fall away from the good world that God intended for us. Sin eventually turns us into miserable creatures who are alienated from God and others.

Far from being free to do as we like, sin becomes a cruel master that will rule our lives, alienate us from God, and prevent us from the true joy of our calling. We find moments of pleasure by indulging in sin, but part of our problem is a lack of information. Letting sin have its way cripples us and leads to long-term consequences we cannot even imagine. We have been made in the image of God to perform good deeds, to enjoy a saving relationship with him through the work of Jesus and the Spirit, and to testify to that love by word and deed.

The Scriptures tell us that sin is not the norm, and that God has in fact given us everything we need to live godly lives (2 Peter 1:3). Christ has carried sin on his body while on the cross, defeated it by rising from the dead, and imparted his life-giving power through the Holy Spirit. Sin is a defeated foe. We don't have to submit to it. In fact, we can live with God in such a way that sin becomes the furthest thing from our minds since we're consumed with the love of God.

A DESIRE PROBLEM

All of that stuff you just read is awesome, right? Doesn't God sound pretty appealing? I'll bet you just read it all, and you're free from sin forever. The goodness of God is practically irresistible after all. Who would go and sin after reading all of that?

Well, the answer is me—and you. Most Christians know this stuff. If you're a Christian who knows a thing or two about Christianity and didn't think I could explain it any better, then you may have skipped that section since you know all of this stuff about sin, salvation, and the facts about living a holy life. And yet, we still go about sinning from time to time. Some of us may live relatively sin free, but for the majority of Christians, sin is tough to shake. We go through our lives crippled by these dark powers that sometimes tug at us in the dark and other times rise to the surface in very public, humiliating ways.

The trouble is that no matter how much information we consume from the Scriptures, we run into a desire problem. We know the truth, but giving in to sin feels good or even inevitable. Like a limp we can't shake, sin attaches itself to us and convinces us that it's part of our lives. And in fact,

---

HOW TO ENJOY GOD

Holiness requires the active pursuit of God. Here are a few simple ways to seek God:

Sit or kneel in silence: Practice sitting still and quiet for at least five minutes. Use a Scripture verse to focus your mind if it helps.

Talk a walk: Let your mind wander and ask the Holy Spirit to guide your thoughts. You may be surprised about where he leads.

Offer thanksgiving: Focus on the things God has given to you and thank him for them. Some prefer to keep a list.

Sing songs of praise: Singing a worship song that praises God's qualities is the best way to turn your attention away from yourself and on to God.

we can't imagine our lives without it. We desire the pleasure, the rush, and the comfort that our sins bring to our lives in the moment, even if we are wracked with disappointment and guilt afterward.

However, sin often sets up shop in our lives because our desires are out of whack—we lack the desire for God. This is something that John Piper addresses in his book *Desiring God*.[1] Piper is right on the mark in saying that we latch on to sin expecting it to bring us pleasure. The problem all along is that we don't have a grasp of true pleasure. God is the source of true and lasting joy. God is not in heaven trying to shut us down from having a good time. In fact, he wants our desires to be oriented in healthy directions that will lead to the good pleasure he has created in our world—pleasure that does not result from being completely consumed with ourselves and our desires.

If you don't know what the joy of the Lord is, I encourage you to take some time to worship and listen. Seek the presence of the Lord. For a set period of time, step away from your leisure activities that are supposed to make you happy. Seek the joy and pleasure that is found in God's presence. Until you know what he has to offer, sin will win almost every time.

AN ENFORCEMENT PROBLEM

So, if you're following me now and you have your facts and desires straight, perhaps you still feel like sin has you under its dark, smudgy thumb. I'm with you on that. It's nice that God wants you to be free and that God is able to offer us greater intimacy and joy than anything we can find here on earth, but don't you wish it was easier to wipe the power and effects of sin from our lives? He has given us everything we need for godly living and we love him deeply, but somehow we still can't connect our facts and desires with reality. Sin is a tricky little bugger.

This is where we need to get spiritual. We are in a spiritual struggle with evil spirits that want to wreck us, as in that guy prowling like a roaring lion seeking to devour us. Peter knew a thing or two about that when Jesus warned him that Satan wanted to tear him apart like harvesting a flimsy piece of grain. There are spiritual forces in this world, demons in fact, who desire to control us, who want nothing more than to become idols that receive our worship and loyalty.[2]

SURVIVAL BETWEEN THE EXTREMES

Ensuring your spiritual survival against sin requires learning to balance between two extremes.

Intellectual Extreme

Advantages: Grounded in the right information.
Disadvantages: Satan knows the Bible too and can work around intellectual arguments.

Spiritual Extreme

Advantages: Grounded in spiritual experience of God and aware of spiritual threats.
Disadvantages: Can lose track of God with misinformation or fail to take advantage of all that God promises in Scripture.

Now, in moving forward we can make two mistakes. One is the intellectual mistake of ignoring this spiritual warfare business because we once saw a preacher on the television wearing a snappy suit who hit a lady over the head with her crutch in order to heal her. I'm from this intellectual tribe, and I've been in churches where I've had to dodge flailing plastic swords and waving flags—stuff that has left me suspicious of spiritual warfare at times. However, whether we have encountered the different, fraudulent, or odd in the past, the Scriptures make it abundantly clear that we are engaged in spiritual warfare that requires God's spiritual resources if we want to win.[3] There are many Spirit-led Christians who have much to teach us about defeating sin, even if we'd feel out of place in their worship services.

The other extreme leaves the intellectual behind and moves more according to emotions, feelings, and "words" from God. If you're really a lost cause, you'll find messages in your toast. That isn't to say that God can't speak through prophetic words or through unusual means. However, we can lose our grip when delving into the spiritual. Some have clung to a supposed "word from the Lord" that only ruined their lives completely.

SURVIVAL TEST

We defeat sin by
  a. memorizing Scripture in the original Greek
  b. getting lost in a prayer labyrinth
  c. relying on the Holy Spirit's power
  d. solitary confinement

We have Scripture and fellow believers to keep us grounded, and while we should fight sin by spiritual means, we should not forget the teachings of Scripture and the wisdom of fellow Christians when we engage in these spiritual struggles.

Keeping these extremes in mind, we can engage in the enforcement of God's will and power over the sin that plagues us. Christ has broken the power of sin with his resurrection, and we have his power at our disposal because the Spirit is in our lives. For starters, we can claim the power of the cross and resurrection over sin and the spirits behind sin fighting against us. Even more than that, we are free from the dragging influence of sin when seeking out God. This is where we will begin to find the victory over sin.

We don't defeat sin by fighting it ourselves. We defeat sin by claiming God's victory as we cling to him. Sin cannot touch us when the Spirit of God is residing in our bodies, his new temple. Therefore, the trick to living in holiness is to seek God with stubborn tenacity whether or not we feel like it. Some sins may break only when we seek prayer from fellow Christians, especially the intercession of those who have been delivered from similar sins. We have the information at hand: God loves us and desires that all people should know him. There are no caveats, no loopholes that exclude you or me. And therefore, we are welcome in his presence because of his Son's work and the Spirit's ongoing influence.

As we enjoy intimacy with God, we can ask him to expose sin for what it is. In other words, as I've prayed about my own struggles with lust and anxiety, they have been revealed as spirits of adultery and fear. Claiming the biblical truth of Christ's victory as my own, I told the spirit of fear and the spirit of adultery to leave because of Christ's victory. While they pester me from time to time, in the years that followed those decisive moments of revelation, I have experienced newfound freedom from these sins that nagged me for years. My time with God that resulted in renewed spiritual insight into my sin struggles brought about a decisive breaking of sin's hold in my life.

FREE AT LAST?

There will be times when we forget about God's victory over sin, slip into our old sinful habits, and then repent. Sin can make inroads even after we have claimed the victory and experienced God on the mountaintops of our lives. We may never be clear from sin's reach until we pass from this world. While we can claim the spiritual victory over sin and break its iron grip on our lives, we can still submit to our old desires. It's like a cancer patient rushing out of the recuperation room to beg the doctor, "Please put that tumor back in, we had so many good times together!"

SIN SURVIVAL STRATEGIES

Here are some ways to break free from sin and thrive as a Christian:

- **Confess your sins to God.** Do you really think you're going to surprise him?
- **Confess your sins to one another.** Break free from sin's controlling guilt, shame, and power.
- **Claim the power of the cross and resurrection.** Jesus conquered sin so that we could enjoy his victory, not just read about it.
- **Tell sin to get out and never return.** Jesus wasn't joking about the authority we have to bind. Learn to use it properly before sin returns to entangle and tie you up again.
- **Stay close to Jesus.** If you're drawing near to Jesus, then you're as far away from sin as you can get.

However, even after breaking sin's hold in some pretty significant ways, I have learned in my experience that there is another step to the process of defeating sin. We can essentially tell sin not only to go away but to never come back. While our ultimate victory comes when we are connected to Christ, our life-giving vine, the Gospels relate stories in which Jesus not only cast out demons, but he instructed them to never come back.

In other words, Jesus took both offensive measures and future defensive measures against evil spirits. In a sense, he bound them. Now, here's where the intellectuals such as myself can become suspicious. I know some of my friends probably think I'm full of it, and these passages have been twisted to mean all kinds of wacky stuff, but Jesus gave his followers authority to bind things on heaven and earth (Matt. 16:19; 18:18). That extends to the spiritual realm when we are dealing with sin.

This is a tough area to speak with complete certainty, but I do know that the light came on for me in my own struggles with sin when I realized I could not only defeat sin through the power of Christ, but also "bind" it by his authority. That doesn't mean I'm a perfect, super-Christian now, but I have never made so much progress in my Christian life until I learned to say to my sin, "Get out, and never come back!"

It's as if I can toss sin out of my life and close the door on it. While that door is shut I am free from its influence as I seek Christ. However, I can still choose to open that door to sin.

CHRISTIAN INSANITY

Many Christians try doing the same thing over and over again to defeat sin and yet they don't experience the freedom that the Scriptures promise. Therefore they keep trying to learn more or to receive more prophetic words. I once heard that insanity is doing the same thing over and over again and expecting different results.

I used to be insane like that. I was insane for far longer than I care to admit.

Over time fellow Christians, books, and particular studies of Scripture helped me try something different. I know what it feels like to struggle with sin for years and years and to rarely see progress. I still have my issues from time to time. I've sat in accountability group meetings where I had to fess up to the same old, same old—especially with my anxiety issues. There's always something new that can freak me out.

That's the worst.

The same old, same old is not what Jesus promised us. We were promised freedom from sin and true joy while surrendering all we have and suffering for the kingdom. However, we won't be able to effectively do any of that fun stuff like leaving everything behind and suffering for Jesus until we get this sin thing defeated. Sin hangs on to us and will catch up to us at one point or another. It will destroy us if we let it hang around like a little puppy that we feed table scraps. Soon the puppy will grow into a wild dog that will tear our homes apart.

We have a lot to learn and much more to put into action. I understand that you may not want to become that guy who shouts "Hal-le-lu-yyyah!" as he whacks someone on the head with an open-handed message from Jesus. I'm also sympathetic to those confident in their feelings and senses about the ways God speaks to them and their fears of becoming a bookish Christian. There are things we could say about both camps, and yet, followers of Jesus need both the information and the practice. We need the constant orientation of God through Scripture, the intimacy of time spent with him, and the application of both offensive and defensive measures against sin.

We can't learn sin away by ourselves and we can't rely on others to give us prophetic words about it. Let's take personal and communal steps to get our facts straight and to engage in a spiritual struggle against sin. Overcoming sin isn't something that has to take place "someday" in the future. We can overcome today. Today is the day of salvation because he has given us everything we need to live holy, godly lives. It may take time. It will not be easy. We will suffer setbacks, but we have the life and power of God at our disposal. Sin is a defeated enemy, and it's time that we treated it as such.

MONEY

GIVE EVERYTHING AWAY AND
THEN TITHE 10 PERCENT TO JEU

I'M NOT A BIG FAN of watching movies. If you're ever paired with me as a partner in a game of Trivial Pursuit, you're going to lose. I'll never know which actor won an Academy Award for his role in *The Thousand Golden Miles* or whatever the hit summer movie was last year. As much as I don't watch movies, I've seen a couple of movies where everyone is really worried about keeping a monster, zombie, or alien out of a room or a spaceship, and then they learn that the creature is already among them. I remember one movie where an alien popped out of a guy's stomach. No matter how hard they tried to keep the alien out of the spaceship, they couldn't stop it from infecting someone and attacking them.

Money is like that. While it's not necessarily out to kill us like a monster or an alien, it has a way of infecting us and the people around us without necessarily being obvious. Even if we can't see it, it's lurking among us. You could say that someone who drives a really expensive car or lives in a mansion probably has some issues to work through with money, but there's a chance you could be wrong. In fact, you could live in a tiny house and have even greater problems with money. That's the thing about money. It sneaks up on you.

Like a ninja.

I'm sure I've seen a ninja movie at some point, but I'm currently drawing a blank.

Money is the kind of threat to our faith that we don't want to acknowledge because we can see all of the good things money does for us. It's not a black-and-white threat. We can always find someone who is more captive to the sway of money. However, money isn't just a material matter. Money is a force that we can use to solve our problems and to build a particular kind of lifestyle. And if you think about the kingdom of God and what Jesus did, you may also see that his kingdom is a particular kind of lifestyle that is often directly in conflict with money. Money is one of the most powerful threats to the Christian faith today. Its power is all the more threatening since many of us are all too quick to dismiss it as a potential problem.

WHY WE HATE TALKING ABOUT MONEY AS AN IDOL

If I asked you, "Do you have a money problem?" there's a good chance you'd reply just like me, "Yeah, I don't have enough." And then we'd have a moment to pause and consider that this most likely isn't the main problem we have with money.

Money is the kind of topic that some churches talk about all of the time, others never talk about, and a few only talk about as a last resort before going broke. There's a good chance that many of the Christians who don't talk about money fear they'll accidentally sound like a church that talks about money all of the time. Money gives Christians fits because we all need it, but we all know it's like a ticking time bomb—a really, really nice looking ticking time bomb that we all want to own (we're up to three similes for money if you're keeping track). In 1 Timothy 6:10, Paul said that "the love of money is a root of all kinds of evil." (That's three similes and a metaphor now.) In the Gospels, the parable of a rich man and a poor man named Lazarus provides a cautionary tale about the snare of money (three similes and two metaphors). The rich young man chose his wealth over Jesus, but Jesus also made the startling request to sell everything he owned. The power of money to distract us or even to take over our lives is clear. In fact, Jesus even went so far as saying that the poor are blessed. Having said all of that, it's clear that money isn't necessarily inherently

SOW SEEDS OF FAVOR!

You may have heard about the health-and-wealth gospel's approach to money where generosity to a ministry will unleash God's financial blessings to those who give. Some "ministers" call this approach to money "sowing seeds of favor" with God. For instance . . .

One minister has an aviation ministry. When he needed new blades for his helicopter, he was excited to send a letter to those who supported his ministry with an "opportunity" to sow seeds of favor. How so? They just had to prop up his ministry with a financial gift toward the helicopter fund. Big bucks were certain to come to his donors if they acted *now*.

I guess you have to spend money to make money.

Forget about seeking first the kingdom of God. Just force God's hand to give you what you want by donating money to a ministry. Get your "favor" today!

evil. Rather, it *can* lead to trouble. If it's a ticking time bomb, it's also a time bomb that we can continually disarm. Let's remember that Jesus was supported by a group of wealthy women. The early church in Acts pooled their resources together to support one another, yet it's clear that plenty of Christians owned homes in order to host meetings. There's no doubt that Priscilla and Aquila had financial means because of their trade as tentmakers.

So while money can become a faith-killing distraction and even a "deity" of sorts, we don't necessarily solve all of our problems by ridding ourselves of money. However, it's clear that money can lead to distractions and far greater problems.

I know that I often fear not having enough money, but should I perhaps spend more time fearing too much money? Should I worry that I'm always worried about not having enough money?

I often tell myself that having a little more money would solve many of our problems and take care of most of the sources of our stress. I rarely consider how a little more of God's kingdom could actually provide a far better resolution to my worries. There is peace and contentment that come from the pursuit of God (1 Tim. 6:6) and treasures that do not rust or decay. Most days, if I'm really honest, it takes a lot of faith to believe that. It's no wonder that money can be such a faith wrecker.

Money, in many ways, can be used to address the very same things that God wants to deal with in our hearts. I certainly need reliable financial provision, but I often want to cut God out of the equation when asking for that provision. Rather than viewing God as my provider and his kingdom as my ultimate goal, I make money into my god, trusting it to provide the security I crave. Money becomes my god that provides comfort.

Money can wreck our faith or at least provide some really problematic distractions. While we can use it well and should never create a once-and-for-all template for how to handle money, failing to discuss it provides room for money to take over.

How then should we deal with money?

JESUS AND MONEY

Am I the only person who wonders how Jesus made ends meet as an itinerant preacher? In terms of money, the Gospels only mention that he had a band of wealthy women who helped meet his needs, but you have to figure that they gravitated toward his cause over time. He had to start somehow, right?

Did he save money before launching his ministry? Did he perform odd jobs on the side? Did he ask the wealthy women to help him? At what point did he have enough money on hand that he put Judas in charge of it?

THE GALILEE GADFLY
HELP WANTED

Wanted: Twelve men of varying intelligence and piety as well as an unspecified number of wealthy women for an open-air preaching tour throughout the land of Israel announcing the arrival of the Messiah. Previous experience not necessary. Training provided. Three-year commitment mandatory.

It's hard for me to imagine Jesus handling money at all. He didn't even have a coin on hand when he spoke about money; he had to ask the Jewish religious leaders on one occasion and Peter on another to bring him a coin.

We already talked a little about how Jesus told a wealthy young man to sell everything he had and give the money to the poor. Another time he criticized a man in one of his stories for building bigger barns to store his bumper crop.

It's clear that Jesus' disciples left their careers behind in order to follow him. Many of the first missionaries and preachers followed in Jesus' footsteps, traveling across the Mediterranean and only working odd jobs when they couldn't raise enough support from the churches they'd planted and continued to encourage and strengthen.

I've always found it curious that Jesus didn't demand that everyone in his audience sell all of their possessions in order to follow him. He didn't command any Roman centurions or officials to sell everything they owned. He regularly visited Lazarus in Bethany, so it's not that he opposed the idea of owning a home.

The "biblical" view of money isn't a template or program we can follow. It's almost like Jesus looked at each person and discerned what made that person tick and what that person needed to do in order to serve God.

In the case of the rich young ruler, Jesus was offering him a chance to be free from his possessions. In the case of Lazarus, Jesus encouraged him and his sisters to use their gifts of hospitality. The disciples couldn't keep their careers as fishermen, tax collectors, and revolutionary wannabes because they had to spend all of their time with Jesus learning to minister like him.

Owning less and working less freed up the disciples for the kind of ministry they were made to perform. Owning more enabled Lazarus to be generous and supportive.

Even a small sum of money can cause as much trouble as a large sum.

The central issue with money for most of us is learning how to manage it. Does it control us or do we control it? We need to regularly disarm the time bomb or lock up the monster. The time bomb may become armed again and the monster may escape, so our survival as Christians requires vigilance and wisdom as we seek to make Christ Lord of our lives and work on holding on lightly to money.

PERFECT TITHING, BROKEN HEARTS

Perhaps the best, most regular givers I can think of for all time would be the Pharisees. They didn't just give a percentage of their money to God. They also tithed from their herb gardens (Matt. 23:23). They were precise and thorough, not holding anything back from God. They were also so consumed with following their strict guidelines that they were unable to see the grip money had on their lives.

Their tithing procedures became a smoke screen that eliminated critical thinking about the hold of money on their lives. So long as they gave 10 percent, they didn't have to think much more about money.

That sounds good to me. I like simple solutions, and tithing 10 percent works. Making a little sacrifice and then doing what I want with the rest is a pretty good bargain. "Ah, ah, ah, God. That 90 percent is for *me.*"

Does God desire only 10 percent today?

This matter of obligations and percentages is really just the tip of the iceberg when it comes to money. Technically speaking, tithing 10 percent is part of the previous covenant with Israel. We now owe Jesus nothing according to the old covenant and everything according to the new covenant.

Regularly giving a percentage of your income is a great little routine that reminds us about our priorities and hopefully loosens the grip of money on our lives. I'm not suggesting that tithing a percentage of your income is wrong or harmful. Rather, tithing a percentage can be used as nothing more than a religious obligation that separates our stuff from God's stuff. If I make a significant amount of money, only tithing 10 percent still leaves me with enough money to get into a lot of trouble. I can still worship money as my god even if I'm giving some of it away. Tithing helps, but that's just the beginning.

SHOULD WE JUST GIVE IT ALL AWAY?

In the case of Christian survival, the central focus with money is whether we are using it to replace God in our lives.

Are we distracted by the things we buy with our money?

Do we make our lives more complicated with money?

Do we use money to solve problems we should entrust to Jesus?

Are we perpetually dissatisfied by how much money we have?

When Jesus spoke with the rich young ruler, he wasn't necessarily providing us with a template for faithfulness, otherwise there would be a lot of people in the New Testament with big problems. Rather, Jesus was offering this young man his own path to discipleship. Attachment to his many possessions held him back, and Jesus offered him the way to freedom and perfection.

The rich young ruler was quite far away from the openhanded detachment from possessions that following Jesus requires. Regular generosity to others is a good way to break the tightfisted grip of possessions on our lives and to incline our hearts toward the needs of others. Perhaps Jesus put him on the fast track. In addition, the discipline of a budget, a spending limit, and regular generosity to a charity that meets important needs can break the hold of money over our lives. As we experience the joy of giving to others, we'll become far less attached to money and more involved in getting to know our neighbors.

> "To be smart enough to get all that money, you must be dull enough to want it."
>
> —G. K. Chesterton[1]
>
> "If a person gets his attitude toward money straight, it will help straighten out almost every other area in his life."
>
> —Billy Graham[2]

Even if money is tight, I've found that generosity is an important way to reorient my focus away from money as god and to refocus on the lordship of Christ. If I can stop looking at money as the solution to my problems, I can free myself to ask a far more important question than, "Do I have enough money?"

WHY I STOPPED ASKING GOD FOR MONEY

Looking at money from where I'm at, I have never had the problem of too much money. I spend the majority of my time trying to sort out ways to earn more money, not how to get rid of it. You won't find me shopping at the mall for fun.

Each time I pray for more money, I find that I'm asking for the worst thing possible.

I want God's solution without a relationship. I want a slot-machine God who dispenses what I want whenever I pull the lever.

I'm basically asking God to help me build my own idol.

"Dear God, only money can save me now, so if you're real and you want me to believe in you, you'd better give me the money I need to solve my problems."

Rather than telling God what I want him to do about my finances, I've found that I need to let go of my circumstance and ask God, "What do you want me to do?"

Once I know what God wants me to do, I'm in a position to obey God and to rely on God to provide what I need.

If money makes the mistake of commodifying everything with a value and price tag, focusing only on what something is worth, serving God is the perfect way to break that cycle. A personal God interacting with people to guide them in their choices pulls us away from the power of money and the hold it can have on our lives. Trusting ourselves to the invisible influence of God is the most financially irresponsible thing you can do in the eyes of investors, but that is the path to freedom and true stability. Money will always come and go. Jobs will be lost. Stock markets will rise and fall.

Money promises control and freedom, but that control and freedom can separate us from God. That control and freedom can be a fleeting illusion as well. If we aren't trusting God to provide what we need, we will fool ourselves into thinking that money is what we really need. Some days I convince myself with that lie.

When I'm hit with anxiety over not having enough money or turn to my slot-machine prayers, that's typically a sign that my trust is in the wrong place. We may end up in situations where money is tight and we have every reason to worry, but we'll never find peace or stability by constantly worrying. I've been there, and I won't say that reaching a point of surrender is easy. However, I've had to confess that I sometimes crave financial stability more than I crave spiritual stability. I know this because my investments in money often receive far more attention than anything else.

The irony of money is that we need to talk about it a lot more, just not in the ways we usually talk about it. I've spent enough time talking about needing more money, but it has taken time to admit my bigger issues with faith, materialism, and generosity. As much as our physical survival is linked to having enough money to buy food and to pay for shelter, our spiritual survival is linked to not letting money become god. When I'm afraid to talk about money with my Christian community but I have no problem asking God for more of it, I should know that something is terribly wrong.

The monster is loose.

The ninja is dangling from the ceiling.

The time bomb is about to explode.

COMMUNITY

WHEN BAD CHURCHES HAPPEN TO GOOD PEOPLE

IT'S BEEN A LONG time coming. One Sunday morning you decide you'd rather stay in your pajamas, drink a leisurely cup of coffee, and check Facebook for the latest celebrity meme instead of going to church. The last straw could have been a judgmental person, a controversial pastor, or the powder creamer at the coffee table—is half-and-half really that expensive?

There are all kinds of ways to justify skipping church. Perhaps you plan to read the Bible a little and even meet a "Christian" friend for lunch. Whatever the justification may be, you completely cut out an organized church meeting from your life for one Sunday.

After that trial run, you realize that your Sunday is actually quite nice without church. You don't have to worry about working in the nursery, dealing with that confrontational couple, or figuring out what the latest worship songs are talking about. Sunday is a day of rest, you tell yourself, so perhaps you should skip church next week too. Heck, why not start a church on Facebook with your friends?

One day you mention to a friend that you're giving up on church and he nods with approval. Before you complete your next sentence, he's already complaining about his church that commits the unforgiveable offense of pairing a boring sermon with bad coffee. Buoyed by this, you tell another friend, and he nearly has a coronary. With a stern look and a wagging finger he warns, "You're risking your salvation by leaving the church."

Can you manage to still be a Christian without attending a church service each Sunday? Besides, isn't the church supposed to be the people rather than the organization?

You don't want to stray away from Jesus if you stop attending church, but you aren't sure you can stomach another Sunday going through the motions. Can you survive without going to church?

I write all of this because that person was me. I ditched organized church for seven years in my twenties, regularly trying to return and regularly disappointed. The role of Christian community has been a particularly important Christian survival topic for me since I've found that Christian community is both the source of many problems and one of the most essential supports for our survival as Christians.

A COFFEE LOVER'S SURVIVAL GUIDE TO CHURCHES

You can tell a lot about a church based on how it serves coffee:

Liturgical: Coffee is never served. These people probably don't read the Bible . . . ever. How else can you explain that?

Mainline: Coffee hour always follows the service, but you need to risk the powder creamer and suspect coffee cake. They read the Bible, but their priorities about coffee aren't in the right place.

Nondenominational Evangelical: The best coffee around, but the greeters and ushers may pour it for you with too much creamer and sugar. They read the Bible, but they'll try to force their beliefs about coffee on you.

Baptist: If your heart survives all of the casseroles at the potluck after the service, you can drink lukewarm coffee. They love the Bible, but only their souls are safe at the potluck.

Charismatic: They'll serve you coffee, but you're doomed if they don't give you a lid for it. They read the Bible, but it may be obscured with coffee stains.

IT'S NOT ME, IT'S YOU: THE SOURCE OF OUR PROBLEMS

OK, so we know that plenty of Christians don't like church, but we need to first tackle why they don't like attending church before we can talk about our survival options. Some problems may be beyond our control, while others could be our fault.

There are churches that pile on the rules and equate Christian living with outward appearance. These are the kinds of churches you read about in Christian memoirs where books are burned, CDs confiscated, PG movies prohibited, ties lassoed around the tender necks of young boys, and girls are dressed in burlap sacks down to their ankles. Woe to anyone who bucks the system.

Other churches are infiltrated by American vices such as greed and cutthroat business tactics. They treat attendees like consumers who must be swayed by marketing campaigns and then mashed into disciple clones who buy into the church's "system." This is not necessarily a sinister plot, but it may feel that way to those who don't want to follow the program.

There also are older ritualistic churches that make you feel like you're at a funeral. You may find the liturgy dry and the relevance on par with a televised croquet match—a televised croquet match with a rain delay.

Whatever your frustrations are with all of these churches, I have particularly good news for you: there are people in all of these churches who most likely share your frustrations. Every time I discuss my own misgivings about what the church has become, I have found tremendous sympathy from regular church attendees. However, in our conversations about church, it's important to avoid crossing the line between personal struggles and criticism of others. The moment we take the offensive against a particular form of church, we create a toxic environment where would-be allies lose sight of the common ground of shared frustrations. Some decide to stick it out in a church and others need to explore another option for fellowship.

There are many different kinds of churches that you may have a valid reason for leaving. It's tough to know how to handle each situation, especially when you have to deal with generational or cultural divisions within a congregation that experience God in ways different from you. You want to be around fellow believers who focus on the central elements of the

gospel, foster healthy Christian community, and encourage one another
to holy living while still reaching out to the community. I mean, what's so
hard about that?

Actually, when you gather a couple hundred people together, many
of whom have strong opinions about how to live as Christians today,
we should be shocked that more ambulances aren't called to church on
Sunday morning. If a group of people deeply cherish their religious beliefs
and practices, we shouldn't be surprised that problems sometimes erupt
within our congregations.

Think about this for a moment: Could you take a cross section of your
neighborhood, gather them in a room for an hour, and pick five songs and
a lecture they would all agree on? Good heavens, just picking one song
they all liked would be hard enough! Community is not for the faint of
heart.

No church is perfect. One preacher I know once said, "If you find the

SURVIVAL TEST

If you don't like the church you're attending you should
    a. write an angry e-mail to the pastor
    b. become a member so you can change it from the
       inside
    c. pray and seek counsel before looking for a different
       church
    d. give up on church forever

When searching for a new church, look for
    a. smoke and lights during the worship service
    b. the largest church possible so that you can remain
       anonymous
    c. a church where you can serve your community, grow
       spiritually, and worship God
    d. a church that gives free iPads to visitors (then call me
       so I can get one too!)

perfect church, don't join it. You'll ruin it." That's so true. I haven't found a perfect church yet. Then again, I'm not the perfect church member. As I've thought about my own reasons for leaving a church, I've had to consider whether the problems I have are my own doing.

I've had to ask myself questions like: Are you expecting your church to solve all of your personal problems? Do you want this church to make you a better disciple? Are you demanding that this church conforms to your own standards and preferences? If so, I'll always find something wrong wherever I go—that is, unless I plant my own church. Then I would have the joy of watching people like me attend the church and demand that I remake it according to their sensibilities. At that point I would finally understand what I put my other pastors through.

Sometimes the problem isn't the church. It's you and me. I know that may be a frightening possibility. Who wants to admit such a problem? Isn't life all the more tidy when we can pass the blame on to others?

In my twenties I had a bit of a meltdown with a church I tried to attend. For one thing, I couldn't stand the music. Standing with my fingers digging into the chair in front of me, I may have audibly sighed as particular songs dragged along from emotional verse, to peppy chorus, and then to another emotional verse.

I remember thinking that church would be much better if they just tweaked the service and the ministries they offered. I kept looking at everything around me that needed to change. Finally, I realized that the biggest problem with that church was me. That church may have had a few problems, but so many other people felt free to worship God there. In fact, it was the greatest thing ever for them. Who am I to tell them what they need?

I needed to step out of that church for a season to get my head on straight. In retrospect, I can see that I simply didn't fit in that church. I had the majority of the problems, expecting a church to cater to me. I needed a major shift in my priorities and values before I could worship God and serve others in a Christian community.

CHURCH VISITOR'S CHECKLIST

During my visit I felt
___ despair
___ freedom

The sermon was based on
___ a movie
___ the Bible

The music focused on
___ my feelings
___ the greatness of God

The offering will
___ build an entertainment wing
___ help the poor, pay the staff

I received
___ a mug
___ prayer for my problems

Church members
___ talk among themselves
___ welcome visitors

The pastor
___ is a rock star
___ leads us to the Rock

Sinners are
___ Democrats
___ welcome

Service is for
___ tennis
___ needs in the community

The tech crew used a
___ PC
___ Mac

If you chose the first option more than half of the time, you may
want to keep looking for a different church.

SURVEYING THE ALTERNATIVES

Now, if you're pretty sure you're not the source of the trouble with this attending church business, what will you do next? Let's remove sleeping in, lounging in slippers all day, or networking with Christians on the Internet from your list of possible options. Christians need to be in some kind of community where they are physically present with fellow believers, eating meals with one another and being physically present to offer comfort and support. While online sites can help us stay in touch with one another, they are not sufficient in and of themselves. Just as posting a note on Facebook is hardly adequate to help a grieving friend who needs meals and a shoulder to cry on, Christian community goes beyond what we can type.

Here's a thought, if you can't handle going to church right now, why not meet with a few Christian friends to pray each week? Keep it simple. Just meet around a meal or some snacks, talk about the things you worry about, and anything else on your mind. Then pray together. Besides, if you're about to leave your church, you're going to need some prayer support. Seek the life and freedom of God, even if it's in a small group for a season.

The most important step in any transition out of church or into a different church is healing past wounds. Far too many wander from one form of church into another without confronting their own issues with rejection, judgment, and unrealistic expectations.

CHURCH CONVERSATION TIPS

If you're not attending church and someone asks, "Are you going to church right now?" you can avoid an awkward conversation by using one of these handy replies:

"I'm fasting from church right now."
"I'm practicing the discipline of solitude."
"I don't go to church, I *am* the church."
"The right church hasn't found me yet."

At the very least these responses should leave your questioners confounded.

After some time meeting in your home you may find that certain options will become more appealing than others. Perhaps your group of friends will want to continue meeting more formally as a home church. Perhaps your prayer group will fizzle and you'll need to find something else. At this point you'll need to prayerfully consider whether you need to suck it up and join an existing church or try out something else with another group outside of traditional church.

CHURCH INC. VS. IN CHURCH COMMUNITY

Let's say you decide to join another church or home church, and now you're trying to figure out what exactly you should look for.

After immersing myself in traditional church meetings for years, spending seven years outside of church, and then finding churches where I could belong, I've attended many different kinds of churches for a variety of reasons. I'll be honest, I hate looking for a church. Visiting a church is a terribly lonely experience where I have often felt conspicuous and hunted by handshakers, yet ignored when it comes to actually having a real conversation with a human being.

Now that I have found a healthy Christian community, I can see what has worked in the past and what hasn't worked. I have a very simple rule about attending church: *You should leave church in better shape than when you arrived.* The change may be small, but meeting with God in community is no small matter. A good church meeting should include some of the following results:

· I focused my attention on the splendor of God.
· I learned something.
· I received prayer.
· I found accountability.
· I served others.
· I was compelled to serve somewhere in my community.
· I was encouraged by fellow Christians.

If a church isn't prompting you to imitate Jesus through holiness, love of neighbors, and service to others, then you need to ask what exactly your church is asking you to do. This is the hardest part about church in general. Once we create an "organization," we will always be tempted to put the organization itself first, forgetting our primary obligations to God, one another, and our neighborhoods.

We will always struggle with trying to preserve the finances of the church, the culture of the church, the reputation of the church, and the programs of the church. That doesn't mean that anarchy is the solution, as anarchy has its own issues. I'm more concerned that the tail begins to wag the dog sometimes. We may start serving our gatherings rather than using our gatherings as an opportunity to serve one another and to be healed before going out to serve our communities.

THE AGONY OF FINDING A CHURCH

I used to really overthink what church should and should not do. Having swung all over the map on church meetings, I've realized that anything from candlelit high liturgy to a group of friends gathering in a living room can serve just fine as a church. In fact, I'm grateful that we have so many different ways to worship God. That can actually be a tremendous asset for us because we can seek out the places where we can find life—sensing the deep, healing breath of the Holy Spirit as we gather together.

Healthy Christian community is essential, but not because skipping church is a sin. The command from the author of Hebrews to not give up gathering together (Heb. 10:25) hardly demands the formation of a nonprofit organization that constructs a building, hires a pastor, and holds a morning and evening service every Sunday with a worship band and a sermon. The author of Hebrews was thinking of the life that comes when we worship God together (most likely with a celebration of the Lord's Supper), encourage one another, and hold one another accountable—the details are wonderfully sparse.

We need to confess our sins to real people. We need friends to pray for us. We need to be challenged to get off our couches and serve our communities. Everything about Christian growth is very specific and personal, and there is no better way to draw near to God than with the support of a community.

Sometimes we turn Christian fellowship into an all-or-nothing matter

WHAT IS THE CHURCH?

Defining a church has been no easy task over the centuries of church history. Here are a few perspectives on the nature of the church:

> "One hundred religious persons knit into a unity by careful organization do not constitute a church any more than eleven dead men make a football team. The first requisite is life, always."
>
> —A. W. Tozer, *Man, The Dwelling Place of God*

> "The perfect church service would be one we were almost unaware of; our attention would have been on God."
>
> —C. S. Lewis, *Letters to Malcolm*

> "The pure ministry of the Word and pure mode of celebrating the sacraments are, as we say, sufficient pledge and guarantee that we may safely embrace as church any society in which both these marks exist. The principle extends to the point that we must not reject it so long as it retains them, even if it otherwise swarms with many faults."
>
> —John Calvin, *Institutes of the Christian Religion*, IV.i.12

> "Let everyone respect the deacons as they would respect Jesus Christ, and just as they respect the bishop as a type of the Father, and the presbyters as the council of God and college of Apostles. Without these, it cannot be called a Church."
>
> —Ignatius of Antioch, *Letter to the Trallians*

> "Suppose there arise a dispute relative to some important question among us, should we not have recourse to the most ancient Churches with which the apostles held constant intercourse, and learn from them what is certain and clear?"
>
> —Irenaeus, *Against Heresies*

where you're either fully involved in a church and its "discipleship system" or you need to abstain from it fully. We need process more than we realize. Throughout the Gospels, we see the disciples and especially the apostles as people who are immersed in a process with Jesus. They frequently missed the point of his stories and failed to step out in faith at crucial moments.

We don't ever read of Jesus saying, "That's it! You're all fired. I'm getting a new group of apostles." Perhaps we imagine Jesus audibly sighing or needing to step away to skim rocks along the Sea of Galilee, but he stuck with his apostles right through Pentecost when he shared his Spirit with them. If it takes us some time to figure out a healthy and life-giving form of church, I think Jesus can stick with us.

From the perspective of American Christianity, there is a strong expectation that good Christians go to an official church service. For everyone who feels like the church has let them down or has caused more problems, these expectations can be suffocating. Sometimes we feel like our only option is escape, and for those who attempt an escape, the condemnation that follows may serve as justification for fleeing a supposedly sinking ship.

When it comes to church, we have so many options available to us. I have seen friends who felt liturgy too constricting and therefore joined a network of house churches. Other friends found that liturgy provided a wonderful order for their worship as an alternative to the three-hymns-and-punt approach in their former churches.

There come times when we need to suck it up and join a community where we can find strong relationships despite other trappings that are less appealing. However, if a particular church becomes difficult to attend, it's not like Christians today lack options. God's Spirit is alive and working in many places, even among small groups who simply meet together for prayer and encouragement. We need the support of our Christian family to help us stay focused on God and to pick us up when we fall down. That is something sleeping in can't do.

NOT ASHAMED OF THE GOSPEL?

DEATH OF A SALES PITCH

YOU WANT EVERYONE you know who isn't a Christian to go to hell. Well, not exactly. You're just afraid to share the gospel with them, which you've heard is just about the same thing as opening the gates of hell for them and giving them a kick on their way down.

Images of bloodstained hands fill your mind whenever you think of the "unsaved" around you. Lady Macbeth has nothing on you. No matter how often you say, "Out, *darn* spot!" you move between guilt and fear because you can't think of a way to share the gospel with these people who supposedly are your friends, colleagues, and family.

You tell yourself that if you truly cared for them, then you'd start some kind of conversation about purpose and meaning in life, tie it to a time when you feared God would banish you to hell, and wrap things up with a whirl through Romans and a salvation prayer that you recite with them word for word.

You've been told that real Christians share their faith and aren't ashamed of the gospel, but you're terrified. I've had anxiety attacks about evangelism . . . while shopping . . . at Walmart. I mean, we could make ourselves insane with evangelism. If every person is an eternal soul who could end up in hell, shouldn't we walk from person to person every minute of every day asking them if they know Jesus?

Perhaps that sounds silly to you, but if we follow some of our evangelism teaching to its natural conclusion, we have a recipe for nervous, pushy, and awkward Christians who try to share their faith whether or not it's the right time or the right person. And in case you hadn't noticed, we have quite a lot of them. If there really is so much at stake—eternal separation from God—then shouldn't we evangelize door-to-door like the Mormons and Jehovah's Witnesses?

What is a faithful follower of Jesus to do? We are commanded to make disciples, but how should we do it and how frequently? Can faithful Christians neglect this charge to make disciples? Are we damning people to hell if we don't share our faith constantly? Are we failures as Christians if we're too ashamed of Jesus to evangelize? Will Jesus deny us one day?

OUR MOTIVATION FOR TALKING ABOUT JESUS

Before you have a panic attack with me, we should begin with some basic Christian principles that tie into talking about Jesus.

My friend Billy had a crush on a girl named Jenny from our college. After we'd graduated, he managed to keep in touch with Jenny, and so whenever we hung out he'd turn into the Jenny newswire. He saw her at the store, she replied to his latest e-mail, and there was a slight chance she

---

THE IMPACT OF OUR MOTIVATIONS

Bad Motivations for Faith Sharing

1. Fear: "If I fail, everyone I know is going to hell."
2. Guilt: "If I don't share the gospel, I won't get their blood off my hands."
3. Duty: "All good Christians need to share the gospel."

Bad Methods of Faith Sharing

1. Fear: "Follow Jesus or you're going to hell forever."
2. Guilt: "Don't turn down the greatest love ever."
3. Duty: "You need to take care of your sin problem."

may actually talk to him on the phone before the next solar eclipse. If he managed to speak with her in person the residual elation made him dizzy. And then one day Billy pulled off a coup. Under the banner of a "college reunion," he managed to convince Jenny to come over to his place for a party with a few friends who were visiting from out of town. He had all kinds of time to hang out with her, and those of us subscribed to the Jenny newswire made sure we kept the other guests entertained while the two of them caught up.

Billy didn't need a lot of coercing to hang out with Jenny, to talk about Jenny, or to organize an event around Jenny. He was smitten with her, loopy beyond the bounds of reason, and willing to organize his day around her if he could spend more time with her. That's what love can do to us.

I can relate to Billy. I've had my own Julie newswire when I've visited friends and Julie isn't there. Love prompts us to talk about the beloved. And that's the most basic first step in talking about Jesus with others: fall in love with God.

It's actually not that hard to do if you think about it. The problem comes when we don't think about it. Christianity is built upon the work of Christ: dying to save us, rising from the dead, and sending his Spirit. As we embrace what these events mean for us today, we can worship him in gratitude and appreciate the selfless love he has given us.

Keep in mind that Jesus spilled his blood on our behalf. This is not just a mystical otherworldly reality. Nails and a spear were literally driven into his body, killing him. It was horrible, violent, and painful, and yet he was so head over heels in love with the people on earth, his treasured creation, that he suffered and then defeated death so that we could live with him in peace and joy.

That's a love worthy of throwing a party.

TAKE ACTION

When we have a clear view of God's love, he'll start to change us. When we are shaped into his kind of people, we'll see things from his perspective.

Motivated by the love of the Father and guided by his Spirit, we are in much better shape to talk about the good news of Jesus. In fact, once we've embraced it fully, we'll struggle to *not* talk about it.

At this point, we've been told that we have to figure out how we're going to discuss Jesus with talkative Sally at the office, David the agnostic brother, or Butch your hunting buddy who only speaks of sports and killing animals. Thankfully we don't all have to be like the gregarious and confident experts who tell us that we can steer every conversation to Christ—though some of us will be all over that approach.

For the rest of us, let me introduce you to Lesslie Newbigin.

Newbigin served as a missionary in India for over thirty years, giving him some serious gospel-sharing chops. In his book *The Gospel in a Pluralist Society* he offers a way forward that may strike some folks as counterintuitive. However, I encourage you to give it a shot. He suggests that the gospel was shared in the book of Acts only as a result of conversations sparked by actions and the Holy Spirit's work. In other words, the Christians were empowered by the Spirit to act, and that prompted people to ask questions.

IN HIS OWN WORDS

Perhaps Lesslie Newbigin explains sharing the gospel best:

The intimate link between the acts and words is made very clear in the mission charge to the twelve as it is given in the tenth chapter of Matthew. At the outset this is simply a mandate to heal and exorcise. . . . Only in verse 7 do we read: "Preach as you go, saying, 'The kingdom of heaven is at hand.'"

. . . Here I may refer again to the point to which I drew attention earlier, namely that almost all the great Christian preaching in Acts are made in response to a question. Something has happened which makes people aware of a new reality, and therefore the question arises: What is this reality? The communication of the gospel is the answering of that question.[1]

Newbigin suggests that we figure out what the Holy Spirit wants us to do, do it, and then answer the questions that come. Get out there and do what God wants, and then trust him to provide the opportunities and results. My current church spends half of its budget on providing family homes for orphans, and that alone sparks plenty of conversations with our neighbors about the gospel. After all, God has adopted us into his family.

Such a nonassertive approach feels so un-American, and of course, that's true. Newbigin was British and lived much of his life as a missionary in India.

His experience and interpretation ring true to me. God places burdens on our hearts, leads us into situations, and brings up conversations that will enable us to speak about him, his love, and his saving work. In addition, as we face adversity with grace, accept scorn with humility, give our money to charities, serve alongside the struggling, and repay evil with good, we'll say quite a lot about the work God is doing in us. It's not always up to us to make gospel-sharing situations happen, but we are responsible for listening to God's lead, displaying the power of God daily, and then acting when opportunities arise. John Cameron, an old farmer friend of Oswald Chambers, once suggested that Chambers speak to his ploughman about Jesus if he got "permission to speak." When Chambers asked what he meant, wondering why Cameron hadn't spoken to the man himself, Cameron replied, "My laddie, if you don't know what the permission of the Holy Ghost is in talking to a soul about salvation, you know nothing about the Holy Ghost."[2]

Sharing the gospel may in fact be more a matter of spending time with God to figure out what to do rather than necessarily forcing a conversation.

This means that we aren't just evangelizing when we try to talk about Jesus. We are always on the clock. This is both a little less intimidating and infinitely more difficult. In other words, you are proclaiming the good news when you respond to a critic with kind words or choose to forgive when cheated. We can show that we are living for the rewards and praise that come from God by allowing the love of God to lift us above the smaller concerns of this world.

KEEP IT SIMPLE

I'm advocating for keeping conversations about and demonstrations of the gospel rather simple, but make no mistake, this is hard work. Talking about Jesus is directly tied into our ability to hear from God and to live under the Spirit's influence daily. We will spend the rest of our lives learning how to cling to him and to allow him to lead and change us daily. Without that foundational relationship with God, talking about Jesus will not be a joyful proclamation of Christ. We'll march off to obey the Scriptures like good soldiers, but we'll often find ourselves looking for ways to talk about the gospel rather than encouraging others to take an active interest by our actions or allowing the conversation to arise naturally from our experiences.

I haven't seen talking about Jesus work all that well when I'm answering a question that no one is asking.

That doesn't mean that we can't initiate activities that will lead to

SHARING THE GOSPEL IN *ESQUIRE* MAGAZINE

What if you wanted to share the gospel with an audience that may have never heard the gospel before? Perhaps you could try contacting a magazine such as *Esquire* and wait for the rejection notice.

Or you could follow Jesus with integrity and wait for *Esquire* to invite you to write it. That's what happened with Shane Claiborne, a founder of The Simple Way and author of *The Irresistible Revolution*. Here's a highlight from his article:

> The more I have read the Bible and studied the life of Jesus, the more I have become convinced that Christianity spreads best not through force but through fascination. But over the past few decades our Christianity, at least here in the United States, has become less and less fascinating. We have given the atheists less and less to disbelieve. And the sort of Christianity many of us have seen on TV and heard on the radio looks less and less like Jesus.[3]

conversations about the gospel. If God is calling you to sit on the street corner with a "TALK TO ME" sign around your neck, go for it. One summer my church farmed a plot in a community garden where we grew food for a local soup kitchen. It wasn't a rousing success, but it did bring up some good conversations. You'd better believe we were there to demonstrate God's kingdom. I'm not growing squash, zucchinis, and eggplants because I like them.

So we have three simple things we need to do: embrace, ask, and act. For starters, we need to embrace the love of God and live daily in relationship with him. As we do this, we can ask, "What would you like me to do today, Lord?" His answers may surprise you. If he leads you to something difficult or unexpected, he'll be sure to provide for the work he has prompted you to do.

We run into problems when we ask God to bless or to provide for what we have decided to do on our own. However, when we step forward based on his prompting we can have confidence that he'll back us up.

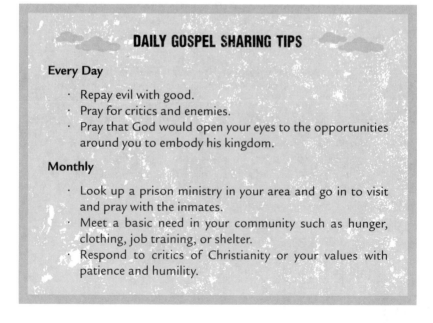

DAILY GOSPEL SHARING TIPS

Every Day

- Repay evil with good.
- Pray for critics and enemies.
- Pray that God would open your eyes to the opportunities around you to embody his kingdom.

Monthly

- Look up a prison ministry in your area and go in to visit and pray with the inmates.
- Meet a basic need in your community such as hunger, clothing, job training, or shelter.
- Respond to critics of Christianity or your values with patience and humility.

I want everyone I know to have a saving relationship with Jesus. There are many different ways we can share the gospel, but it should never be motivated out of guilt or duty. The good news of God's loving salvation should also never be forced upon anyone. Christianity is relational and rooted in love. Some folks can take the direct approach, while others will be better able to engage in service to the poor as a means of proclaiming the gospel. Both are ways of saying to the world that God has inaugurated a new way forward in Christ.

Guilt and fear have been conquered on the cross, and therefore they have no place in sharing the gospel. God loves us, Jesus is Lord, and we are saved through his death and resurrection. The "darn spot" has been removed from us, and that is something we can talk about.

THE HOLY SPIRIT

FLAMES OF TONGUE-TIED FIRE

MEETING CHARISMATIC Christians for the first time sent my faith into a nosedive. It wasn't their fault. I brought all of the insecurity and unrealistic expectations.

The problem that comes up when you meet people who hear prophetic messages from God, heal the sick, and speak in tongues is this: they highlight in bold the passages in the Bible where there is a manifestation of the Holy Spirit and remind you of how little faith you have. The Holy Spirit and miraculous signs are woven throughout the New Testament. Paul casually mentions that he speaks in tongues more often than the Corinthians, instructs prophets on how to share their messages in good order, and performs timely miracles when they are needed most. It all reads as so normal. And yet it's all abnormal for many of us today. I've spent more than my fair share of time wondering, *What's wrong with me if I'm not experiencing these outward gifts?*

The most difficult passage for me to read in Lauren Winner's book *Girl Meets God* covers speaking in tongues. As she learns about speaking in tongues, she asks God for the gift and tries to focus on it. "*Tongues, tongues, tongues,*" she tells herself. "*Tongues, tongues, tongues.*"[1] I cringe both because I know how she feels and because I can sense the failure that is coming her way. While never figuring out tongues and other gifts of the Spirit isn't all

Should you venture into a charismatic church service, either by mistake or on purpose, here's a crash course on the lingo:

Common Charismatic Words and Phrases

Manifestation: Since charismatics believe that God can "show up" in a real way that we can sense, they speak of God's presence or intervention as a manifestation.

Breakthrough: When praying, charismatics often ask God for a breakthrough. The implication is they're uncertain or feel stuck. The holdup could be physical or spiritual. Either way, a prayer for breakthrough typically involves waiting on God to provide direction.

Anointing: Much like a king or priest would be anointed for a sacred duty in the Old Testament, charismatics speak of God's blessing and empowerment for ministry. The main difference is that oil isn't mandatory for an "anointing" today, which means you get 100 percent anointing with 0 percent mess.

Bind/Loose: Binding and loosing spirits and other negative things is a big part of the charismatic world, and for good reason. Jesus promised Peter that he would be able to bind and loose spiritual powers on earth and in heaven. Charismatics take that promise as a direct message for them. Don't worry, you'll never be "literally" bound and then loosed.

Revival: We all know what a revival is, but some charismatic churches believe a great revival precedes the end of the world. In other words, if you want Jesus to return, make a revival happen. This isn't just a "revival" where a large group of people return to God. Such a revival is a sign from above that the gospel is reaching to the ends of the earth and the end is near. You may also hear the phrase "For such a time as this," which points toward the same thing: *End times carnage is coming soon.* Yay, revival!

that catastrophic for Winner's faith, it has been difficult for me. I almost lost my faith when I encountered charismatic gifts.

Let's face it, if you have never experienced spiritual gifts before and then you learn that God has intended for you to experience them all along, you're left with some hard questions. Why am I not experiencing these "normal" gifts that every other Christian is supposed to have? Has God ruled me out in some way? Do I not have enough faith? Am I really a Christian?

Perhaps these questions strike you as absurd or perhaps they strike you as logical.

Spiritual gifts such as tongues, prophecy, and miracles have proven quite helpful for some Christians. They're just normal parts of being a Christian for them. For others they take on an inflated role where having or not having them becomes the mark of whether or not you're a Christian. For me, they became a source of insecurity and doubt. What did it mean if I didn't "manifest" any spiritual gifts?

From what I can tell, Christians in America especially struggle to figure out how the Holy Spirit fits into their personal lives and into their congregations. For those who believe in a present and active Holy Spirit, there is a temptation to abuse or to control the Holy Spirit. For those who believe in a more peripheral Holy Spirit, there is a danger of relying on their own wisdom and cultural standards. They may only avail themselves of a small part of what the Scriptures promise believers.

I have saved this topic for the end of this book because it is one of the most important topics for Christians to figure out if they want to survive. The Holy Spirit enables us to live in holiness, to experience intimacy with God, to serve others, and to pass along blessings to others. While discipleship often focuses on introducing Christians to the correct doctrines and some essential practices such as Bible study and service to others, it's not all that easy to "teach" someone how to dwell in the Holy Spirit and to then live through the Spirit's power.

WHY WON'T THE HOLY SPIRIT COME?

The Holy Spirit presented the perfect storm for a Baptist like me.

I knew that biblically speaking the Holy Spirit is essential for the Christian faith. It is quite another matter to figure out a place for the Spirit in American evangelical churches that tend to emphasize strategic planning, Bible teaching, and a Spirit functioning in the background without necessarily manifesting in ways we can feel and observe, sort of like God being behind the scenes but never mentioned by name in the story of Esther. I learned to pray with the uneasy expectation that God may do something, but if God did too much, something would be wrong.

The irony is that I was most resistant to the Holy Spirit when I was most concerned with following the Bible literally. If I took the Bible seriously, I should have walked around putting my hands on sick people and praying for them to be healthy again.

Instead, I just prayed for wisdom or comfort or whatever I could think of saying that sounded good.

Forget about healing the lame. My Christianity was lame. I wanted to follow Jesus, but I also didn't know what to do about the Holy Spirit who figured so prominently in the New Testament. Where does someone begin with the Holy Spirit?

I learned about the Holy Spirit, but I only really knew how to "experience" the Bible. The more I studied the Bible, the more convinced I became that I needed a deeper experience of the Holy Spirit.

Beyond what I learned, I started meeting Christians who had dramatic experiences of the Holy Spirit. Some healed others, some had prophetic words, some had experienced emotional healing, some had dreams and visions, and some spoke in tongues.

I knew these people. They were not deceptive. Something supernatural was happening, and it lined up with what I read in the Bible. That left me with a disturbing question.

Why am I not experiencing the Holy Spirit?

As a good Baptist I was determined to take the Bible "at its word." I was going to ask God for the Holy Spirit. I read in the Bible that people prayed for the Holy Spirit and BOOM!

If the Bible was true, this had to work. Why would God let me doubt him?

Why didn't the Holy Spirit come when I asked?

My faith took a critical nosedive.

At my best I was uninformed and inexperienced with the Holy Spirit. At my worst, I came dangerously close to completely losing my faith because I didn't understand how the Holy Spirit works. I had this nagging suspicion

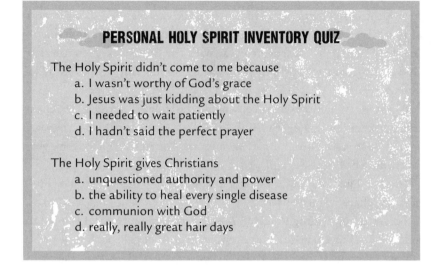

PERSONAL HOLY SPIRIT INVENTORY QUIZ

The Holy Spirit didn't come to me because
a. I wasn't worthy of God's grace
b. Jesus was just kidding about the Holy Spirit
c. I needed to wait patiently
d. I hadn't said the perfect prayer

The Holy Spirit gives Christians
a. unquestioned authority and power
b. the ability to heal every single disease
c. communion with God
d. really, really great hair days

over the years that acknowledging a bigger Holy Spirit suddenly made my faith a complicated mess.

I was completely right about something at last.

Once I believed in a present Holy Spirit, I had so many questions and a pile of doubts and fears to sort through.

Every time I sat down to pray, I felt like my faith was being put to the test. God is supposed to show up if I have the Holy Spirit, so what does it mean if the Holy Spirit doesn't show up?

I expected to feel something. I'd seen people pray and have dramatic encounters with the Spirit—weeping, laughing, or experiencing a deep sense of peace. Others received specific direction from God. I saw signs that God was doing something for other people.

When I prayed and asked for the Holy Spirit to come, I felt nothing. My frustration and doubt grew.

The hardest part about going from noncharismatic to charismatic in my belief and practice was sorting out the place of the Spirit in my everyday Christian practices, whether that was reading the Bible, praying quietly, or praying for someone else.

For a season, I dreaded sitting down to pray since I feared I would not experience the presence of the Holy Spirit and spend the rest of my day questioning my faith and the existence of God.

I have very little patience for anyone who makes this Holy Spirit stuff sound simple. Some of us have really struggled with this while having the best intentions. I wanted to take it seriously, but I also didn't know how it all worked.

As is often the case in Christianity, blueprints and expectations led me astray.

For instance, my father-in-law prayed for me once and said that he sensed the Holy Spirit coming to fill me up. I didn't doubt him, but I also didn't feel anything happen. I didn't even say a single word in a tongue.

What gives?

After stumbling around with the Holy Spirit for a few years, I've learned that the outward manifestations or anything I feel is far from the point. Really, really far from the point in fact.

WAITING ON GOD

We have an instant culture with fast food, high-speed Internet, zippy smart phones, microwave dinners, and super highways that let us move at top speeds. You can't turn the Holy Spirit into an instant spiritual fix. You don't take the Holy Spirit with a glass of water and enjoy your afternoon after filling up.

I had to wait and persevere. I had to let others pray for me. I had to open myself up to however God wanted to speak to me or through me.

404 HOLY SPIRIT ERROR

We're sorry, but the Holy Spirit download into your Christian life has failed. Please take the following steps:

- Sit extra quiet and pray extra hard.
- Seek your pastor for tech support.
- Google it.
- Reboot your Christianity by responding to the altar call this Sunday.

Learning to sit and wait without expectation has helped me take some positive steps with the Holy Spirit. Rather than focusing on what I expected to happen or what God's inaction meant about my faith, I finally hit a place where I just waited to see what God would do.

In other words, I don't ask God for anything "Holy Spirit related" unless I feel peace about making that request. I don't know how the mechanics of this work or if there are any rules. I just know that prayer isn't this big grab bag that we can access any old time. Prayer is about getting on the same page with God, waiting for his prompting, and then moving in the direction he leads with enough faith to believe he can accomplish something in or through you if he gave you the prompting in the first place.

We can wallow in uncertainty and guilt when we fail to take the Holy Spirit into account when people challenge us to do "big things" for God or challenge us to ask God for specific things like healing a disease or money for a massive bill. We can dream up all kinds of tests for God that make sense in light of Scripture without actually knowing where and when God wants us to step out in faith. Small or big risks are not about faith unless God gives you the vision. Christian obedience isn't about making a plan on our own and begging God to make it happen. I've learned that I need to listen and hear God for direction before taking a step in faith.

There is tremendous freedom in waiting with hands open, believing that God can show up if he so pleases or that I could receive a word from God; that I can sit in the presence of God or sit in silence.

For all of the times in the Bible that we see God show up, there are plenty more that pass by unnoticed where God doesn't give any messages or do anything of note. This is how we ended up with psalms of lament: "How long, LORD? Will you forget me forever? How long will you hide your face from me?" (Ps. 13:1).

Once I started to open myself up to the Spirit's voice without asking for something specific, I started to hear things.

SPIRITUAL WARFARE IS WEIRD BUT REAL

Any time I explain the Holy Spirit to someone who doesn't have a grid for it, I have a hard time putting my finger on what exactly I hear or how

I know I've heard the Spirit. More often than not, I get a sense that something is true and that I need to pray about it or act on it.

Most of the time nowadays, there's a result of some sort that confirms I'd heard correctly.

In praying for myself and others, the Holy Spirit sometimes gives me a specific thing to pray about. On one occasion I was praying about our marriage, and the Holy Spirit spoke right to my laziness in a certain situation.

That doesn't happen all of the time, and honestly, I don't make myself hear these things. I also don't think my wife is hiding behind the couch, whispering things while I pray. I just wait for God to do something. Sometimes it comes after a lot of waiting and sometimes it comes before I've even started to pray and sometimes, many times, I don't hear anything.

Perhaps the most startling thing I've heard is to pray about spiritual battles. In other words, I hear that I need to pray against a spirit of some sort in a person's life. I'll bet that may either alarm or confuse some folks. Do we really have demons or evil spirits trying to make us sin?

The answer I've found is this: sometimes.

I've received the profound sense that I needed to pray for certain couples "right now." It is awkward and a bit strange, but if I listen to that urge, God brings up something that I need to pray about.

I can't explain this. I just know that sometimes there are evil forces in this world trying to undo relationships, spiritual growth, and other good things. Other times sin in a person's life is more of a personal choice. We can't blame everything on evil spirits, but they're out there and sometimes they're directly involved.

While demons aren't crawling all over the pages of the New Testament, Jesus spent a good deal of time casting them out of people. Jesus also warned Simon Peter that Satan was certainly out to get him: "Simon, Simon, Satan has asked to sift all of you as wheat. But I have prayed for you, Simon, that your faith may not fail" (Luke 22:31–32). That sounds pretty intense to me. It's like Satan is almost prowling for the kill like a, well, lion. At least, Peter took it that way: "Be alert and of sober mind. Your enemy the devil prowls around like a roaring lion looking for someone to devour" (1 Peter 5:8). Even Paul was tormented by a messenger from Satan (2 Cor. 12:7). Paul also warned Timothy of deceptive spirits and demons (1 Tim. 4:1), and James warned about demonic "wisdom" (James 3:15).

AN ARGUMENT WITH DEMONS

Abba Anthony was one of the earliest desert fathers. He lived in simple poverty in the arid outlands of Egypt around the fourth century. Anthony frequently argued with demons in his lonely desert caves and outposts. In addition, the people from a nearby city traveled to see this holy man so often that Anthony ventured deeper into the wilderness to live in an abandoned military outpost. As daring pilgrims ventured to Anthony's fortress, they stood outside the walls and heard him arguing with unseen spirits. Those who cried out in terror were encouraged by the gentle monk to make the sign of the cross and to pray.

Last time I checked, I don't know anyone who argues with demons, but that doesn't mean spiritual forces aren't trying to keep us from praying. In fact, some of my most dramatic steps forward have come from asking God to identify the barriers in my spiritual growth. There are plenty of hucksters who distort spiritual warfare, but if we treat all talk of spiritual warfare as phony, we are leaving ourselves exposed to attacks from a determined and resourceful enemy.

We can't blame our every failure on demons prowling about, but ignoring them would require chopping out quite a bit of the New Testament, especially Paul's warning that we are indeed fighting against spiritual forces (Eph. 6:12). We shouldn't jump to conclusions about spiritual forces in the world every time something bad happens,[2] but they're present and diametrically opposed to Christians. Such a possibility should make us all the more dependent on God to provide wisdom and discernment.

The good news is that God's people are both protected and guided by the Holy Spirit (see 1 John 4:4 and John 16:13). Christ's victory on the cross also stands as an unmistakable victory over evil. Paul wrote, "Having disarmed the powers and authorities, he made a public spectacle of them, triumphing over them by the cross" (Col. 2:15). While evil is certainly still present in the world, the cross has already decided the battle between good and evil. In fact, John in Revelation reminds us that Satan is actually chained down. While we could argue about what this exactly means, it sure seems that Paul and John both believed that Satan and his minions have been defeated by the cross and are severely limited.

From what I've seen, "spiritual warfare" generally isn't too dramatic, at least not often in our "enlightened" Western culture—though I've heard some stories that prove the exception to that. Prayers shared in the midst of spiritual warfare aren't necessarily supposed to resemble an exorcism. In fact, I wonder if we sometimes add the drama. Besides, I can't imagine that anyone is able to discern the influence of an evil spirit on his or her own. The guidance of the Holy Spirit is essential here. If you've sensed that the Spirit has revealed something to you about spiritual warfare, then it makes sense to rely on the Holy Spirit to illuminate the next step forward as well.

CORRECTING THE ABUSE OF SPIRITUAL GIFTS

Jesus promised his followers that they would do greater works than he had done. However you interpret that, we can all agree that dramatic and powerful actions should follow. Jesus was pretty impressive after all.

However, with great authority and power comes the possibility of abuse.

In fact, there are plenty of pastors and ministry leaders I know whom I'd almost rather not see with the spiritual gifts of discernment or prophecy. Who knows what a leader determined to maintain power and control could do with gifts like that?

If God has truly given you something, then you should expect it to resemble the character of Jesus. The manifestation of gifts should always be in a spirit of love. They should mend and heal, encourage and restore.

If you want gifts, you're starting in the wrong spot.

The desert fathers and mothers went into the wilderness in search of God. They found God, but they found a whole lot more than God. They experienced manifestations of God's power, but they didn't seek out these manifestations of God's power. Knowing God intimately first and foremost, they kept their gifts in perspective, not giving them any greater credence than warranted. They recognized that intimacy with the risen Christ meant more than any ability to heal or prophesy.

When Paul wrote to the Corinthians, he warned them about seeking the more "spectacular" gifts that appeared to be more impressive. Instead, he challenged them to seek a gift like prophecy that could be used to build up other believers. I can personally attest that the times God gives me a word of encouragement for someone is one of the most fulfilling things I can ever do. Speaking blessing and hope over someone is particularly hopeful in our culture that values snark and provides plenty of opportunities to tear down others.

I don't want anyone to read this chapter and go into a panic attack over not having enough or the right spiritual gifts or needing to experience God in a particular way. The active presence of the Holy Spirit in your life can be both appealing and frightening. There are some times when I sit down to pray, and I struggle with "relaxing" in God's presence.

I want something to happen! Why isn't something happening?

Cue panic.

The Holy Spirit isn't about proving something to ourselves, others, or God. You can't make God do anything, but you can enter God's presence with open hands.

The best advice I can give someone about the Holy Spirit is to seek out someone who can provide support and guidance. The Holy Spirit is God's gift to you, but it's not easily received because we have so much junk in our lives that distracts us and makes it hard to connect with God. And the digital age may be making it even harder.

Over the years I've learned what it feels like to have a quiet spirit before God. That doesn't mean I'm better at quieting my spirit necessarily. It just means I can spot a manic mind much easier and at least work on stilling myself before God.

The Spirit will dramatically change our lives and put us in tune with God in new ways. The presence of the Spirit is even worth having a crisis of faith over.

OUR MYSTICAL MARRIAGE WITH CHRIST

We have covered a bunch of topics related to survival as Christians. There are so many ways our faith can grow weak, weary, or uncertain. Perhaps you're even thinking of a topic I've overlooked.

There's only one thing I know for certain about Christianity. In fact, it's the only way I know to make it work: stay close to Jesus.

> "Define yourself radically as one beloved by God. This is
> the true self. Every other identity is illusion."
>
> Brennan Manning, *Abba's Child*[3]
>
> In a sermon preached in 2007, Brennan Manning said the fol-
> lowing, which in many ways sums up his message about God's
> love for us:
>
> > The god of so many Christians I meet is a god who is too
> > small for me. Because he is not the God of the Word, he
> > is not the God revealed by and in Jesus Christ, who this
> > moment comes right to your seat and says I have a word
> > for you: "I know your whole life story. I know every skel-
> > eton in your closet. I know every moment of sin, shame,
> > dishonesty, and degraded love that has darkened your
> > past. Right now I know your shallow faith, your feeble
> > prayer life, your inconsistent discipleship, and my word
> > is this: I dare you to trust that I love you just as you are
> > and not as you should be, because you're never going to
> > be as you should be."[4]

Some are clinging to the Bible like a life preserver.

Others are kicking the tires of their faith, unsure whether it can last.

Plenty of others have reached a place of peace and acceptance with what they know and don't know.

Wherever you're at, never forget the simple message that Jesus loves you. He saved you and wants to meet with you because he loves you. This love is higher, wider, and deeper than we can fathom. Sometimes we talk so much about God saving wretched sinners like us that we forget Jesus' words to his disciples apply to us as well: "Greater love has no one than this: to lay down one's life for one's friends" (John 15:13).

The Bible alone can't save you.

The answers to your doubts about the Bible won't save you.

Giving away your possessions won't save you.

Stay close to Jesus. His love will bind you to him and carry you when answers fail.

You can't learn anything that will replace the real presence of Jesus in your life.

We can't think or work our way closer to Jesus.

My pastor says that he often sees people hit a wall at one point where they can't think their way closer to Jesus, and they either become agnostic, rejecting a God they can't understand, or become mystics, which is a way of saying they lean heavily on the experience of being united with Christ through the Spirit. From the Old Testament through the New Testament, our relationship with God is regularly described as a committed, loving marriage.

If this book has tried to do anything, it's clearing a path for your faith—getting rid of any obstacle that could keep you from drawing closer to Jesus.

The only way I know to stay close to Jesus is to trust in the presence of the Holy Spirit each day. It's a mystery that we can only reach out for, trust in, and wait on. The Spirit will sustain you and keep you focused on the author and finisher of your faith, the one and only foundation who is unmovable, unconquerable, and unwavering in his passion for you, his beloved.

NOTES

CHAPTER 1: PRAYER

1. "Frequency of Prayer among Evangelical Churches" (pie chart), in "Portrait of Evangelical Churches" (under Beliefs and Practices select "Evangelical Churches"), Pew Research Religion & Public Life Project, accessed July 3, 2013, http://religions.pewforum.org/portraits.

2. Henri J. M. Nouwen, *The Way of the Heart: Desert Spirituality and Contemporary Ministry* (New York: HarperCollins, 1981), 73–76.

3. See "The Divine Hours," Vineyard Church Ann Arbor, accessed July 4, 2013, http://annarborvineyard.org/tdh/tdh.cfm.

4. Frederick Buechner, *The Magnificent Defeat* (New York: HarperCollins, 1966), 130.

5. Shona Crabtree, "Book Uncovers a Lonely, Spiritually Desolate Mother Teresa," *Christianity Today*, August 30, 2007, http://www.christianitytoday.com/ct/2007/augustweb-only/135-43.0.html. See also Mother Teresa, *Come Be My Light: The Private Writings of the Saint of Calcutta*, ed. Brian Kolodiejchuk (New York: Doubleday, 2007).

6. Daniel Trotta, "Letters Reveal Mother Teresa's Doubt About Faith," *Reuters*, August 25, 2007, http://in.reuters.com/article/2007/08/24/idINIndia-29140020070824.

CHAPTER 2: THE BIBLE

1. There are many assumptions about "biblical manhood" and men's ministry that simply don't stick to many men who follow Jesus. See my guest post for Sarah Bessey titled "In Which Some Guys Do Not Want to Kill Stuff at Mens' Ministry," *Sarah Bessey* (blog), October 4, 2011, http://sarahbessey.com/in-which-some-guys-do-not-want-to-kill/.

2. See Rachel Held Evans, *A Year of Biblical Womanhood: How a Liberated Woman Found Herself Sitting on Her Roof, Covering Her Head, and Calling Her Husband "Master"* (Nashville: Thomas Nelson, 2012).

3. The Hebrew word *yom* that we translate "day" can just as easily mean an undetermined period of time. While it's not necessarily wrong to believe in a young earth created in six twenty-four-hour days, the Hebrew text does not require that kind of reading and may in fact be more accommodating to translating "days" as "periods."

4. Frederick Buechner, *Secrets in the Dark* (New York: HarperCollins, 2006), 269.

CHAPTER 3: VIOLENT BIBLE STORIES

1. Shalom Auslander, *Foreskin's Lament: A Memoir* (New York: Riverhead Books, 2007), 1.

2. David T. Lamb, *God Behaving Badly: Is the God of the Old Testament Angry, Sexist, and Racist?* (Downers Grove, IL: InterVarsity Press, 2011).

CHAPTER 4: DELIVER US FROM EVIL

1. David Roach, "Research: Americans Turn to God and Generosity After Natural Disasters," *Facts&Trends*, May 28, 2013, http://factsand trends.net/2013/05/28/research-americans-turn-to-god-generosity -after-natural-disasters/#.U0QDpiiRZtc.

2. Frederick Buechner, *The Return of Ansel Gibbs* (New York: Alfred A. Knopf, 1958), 303.

3. C. S. Lewis, *A Grief Observed* (1961; repr., San Francisco: HarperCollins, 2001), 18–19.

4. Ibid., 48.

5. My apologies to Sam and Dean Winchester from the TV series *Supernatural*.

CHAPTER 5: HELL

1. Francis Chan and Preston Sprinkle, *Erasing Hell: What God Said About Eternity and the Things We Made Up* (Colorado Springs: David C Cook, 2011).

2. N. T. Wright, "Wright on Hell and Bell," *Alter Video Magazine*, The Work of the People, May 23, 2011, http://www.theworkofthepeople .com/nt-wright-on-hell-and-bell (originally accessed July 31, 2013 on YouTube, but video is no longer available there).

3. See Bruce's letter to John Stott quoted in Timothy Dudley Smith, *John Stott: A Global Ministry* (Downers Grove, IL: InterVarsity Press, 2001), 354–55.

4. C. S. Lewis, *The Great Divorce* (1946; repr., San Francisco: Harper-Collins, 2009); C. S. Lewis, *The Problem of Pain* (1940; repr., New York: HarperCollins, 2009), 129.

5. Theophilus of Antioch, "10.2 Theophilus of Antioch on Conditional Immortality," *The Christian Theology Reader*, 4th ed., ed. Alister E. McGrath (Malden, MA: Wiley-Blackwell, 2011), 537.

6. Irenaeus wrote, "And therefore he who shall preserve the life bestowed upon him, and give thanks to Him who imparted it, shall receive also length of days for ever and ever. But he who shall reject it, and prove himself ungrateful to his Maker, inasmuch as he has been created, and has not recognised Him who bestowed [the gift upon him], deprives himself of [the privilege of] continuance for ever and ever." *Against Heresies*, book 2, chap. 34, accessed July 13, 2013, http://www.newadvent.org/fathers/0103234.htm. See also Irenaeus, *Against the Heresies*, Book 2, trans. Dominic J. Unger, Ancient Christian Writers 65 (Mahwah, NJ: Paulist Press, 1992), 81. However, it should be noted that some think Irenaeus did in fact define eternal punishment as eternal conscious torment.

7. Justin Martyr, *Dialogue with Trypho the Jew*, chap. 5, accessed July 13, 2013, http://www.earlychristianwritings.com/text/justinmartyr-dia loguetrypho.html.

8. I've capitalized the place name *Sheol*, which I've also consistently italicized for emphasis, to represent the Hebrew term *she'ol*.

9. R. H. Charles, *The Apocrypha and Pseudepigrapha of the Old Testament in English*, vol. 2., *Pseudepigrapha* (Oxford: Clarendon Press, 1963), 205–6, https://archive.org/stream/apocryphapseudep02char#page /204/mode/2up.

10. I've capitalized the place name *Gehenna*, which I've also consistently italicized for emphasis, to represent the Greek term *geenna*.

11. In this and the following quotations from the Gospels, I have adapted the Scripture text by inserting the place name *"Gehenna"* in place of "hell" (*geenna*) to indicate more clearly the use of this term in the original Greek and to show the relative infrequency of this term in the New Testament (eleven times in the Gospels, twelve times total).

12. Barclay makes this case in his autobiography where he comes out in support of universalism. While I do not intend to argue in favor of or against his interpretive point of view, I bring him up because he further illustrates the complexities we face when translating a language and trying to take into account the range of meaning for individual words. In this case we are dealing with our assumptions about what kind of punishment Matthew had in mind. See *William Barclay: A Spiritual Autobiography* (Grand Rapids: Eerdmans, 1977), 65–67.

13. F. F. Bruce quoted in Edward Fudge, *The Fire That Consumes: A Biblical and Historical Study of the Doctrine of Final Punishment* (Fallbrook, CA: Verdict Publications, 1982), vii.

14. I've capitalized the place name *Hades*, which I've also consistently italicized for emphasis, to represent the Greek term *hadēs*.

15. N. T. Wright, *For All the Saints? Remembering the Christian Departed* (Harrisburg, PA: Morehouse, 2003), 45–46. Available online as "Rethinking the Tradition," accessed May 29, 2013, NTWrightpage.com, http://ntwrightpage.com/Wright_Rethinking_Tradition.htm.

CHAPTER 6: ERRORS IN THE BIBLE?

1. "P46 in Perspective," Reading the Papyri, web-based project hosted by the University of Michigan Papyrus Collection, accessed August 1, 2013, http://www.lib.umich.edu/reading/Paul/perspective.html.

2. Daniel Wallace, "Earliest Manuscript of the New Testament Discovered?" *DTS Magazine*, February 9, 2012, http://www.dts.edu/read/wallace-new-testament-manscript-first-century/.

3. Kathryn Schulz, "On Being Wrong," TED Talks, filmed March 2011, posted April 2011, http://www.ted.com/talks/kathryn_schulz_on_being_wrong.html.

4. Kathryn Schulz, *Being Wrong: Adventures in the Margin of Error* (New York: Ecco, 2010), http://beingwrongbook.com/synopsis.

5. Ehrman makes this argument at length in his audio teaching series on the New Testament from The Great Courses: Bart D. Ehrman, *The New Testament*, Great Courses (Chantilly, VA: Teaching Company, 2003), DVD, http://www.thegreatcourses.com/tgc/courses /course_detail.aspx?cid=656.

6. For more about education in the ancient Near East and the role of rote memorizations, see Andrew E. Hill, "Education in Bible Times," *Baker's Dictionary of Evangelical Theology*, accessed July 12, 2013, http://www.biblestudytools.com/dictionaries/bakers-evangel ical-dictionary/education-in-bible-times.html.

CHAPTER 7: THE BIBLE AND CULTURE

1. Stephen Arterburn and Jack Felton, *Toxic Faith: Experiencing Healing from Painful Spiritual Abuse* (1991; repr., Colorado Springs: Shaw, 2001).

2. David Johnson and Jeffrey VanVonderen, *The Subtle Power of Spiritual Abuse: Recognizing and Escaping Spiritual Manipulation and False Spiritual Authority within the Church* (1991; repr., Minneapolis: Bethany House, 2005).

3. Here's an article that explains the ways that cultures shape our identity and the complexity of interpreting the Bible across cultural divisions and over the course of time: Roy E. Ciampa, "Ideological Challenges for Bible Translators," *International Journal of Frontier Missions* 28, no. 3 (Fall 2011): 139–48, http://www.ijfm.org/PDFs_ IJFM/28_3_PDFs/IJFM_28_3-Ciampa.pdf.

CHAPTER 8: NO DOUBT?

1. Frederick Buechner, *Secrets in the Dark* (New York: HarperCollins, 2006), 124.

CHAPTER 9: APOCALYPSE NOW?

1. N. T. Wright, *Surprised by Hope: Rethinking Heaven, the Resurrection, and the Mission of the Church* (New York: HarperCollins, 2008), 120.

2. R. Todd Mangum and Mark S. Sweetnam, *The Scofield Bible: Its History and Impact on the Evangelical Church* (Colorado Springs: Paternoster, 2009), 169.

3. H. A. Ironside, *The Great Parenthesis: Timely Messages on the Interval between the 69th and 70th Weeks of Daniel's Prophecy* (Grand Rapids: Zondervan, 1943), 23.

CHAPTER 10: SIN ADDICTION

1. John Piper, *Desiring God: Meditations of a Christian Hedonist*, rev. ed. (Colorado Springs: Multnomah, 2011).

2. See 1 Cor. 10:19–20; compare Rev. 19:20.

3. See, for example, 2 Cor. 10:4; Eph. 6:10–19; 1 Thess. 5:8.

CHAPTER 11: MONEY

1. G. K. Chesterton, *A Miscellany of Men* (1912; repr., West Valley City, UT: Walking Lion Press, 2006), 85.

2. Harold Lawrence Myra and Marshall Shelley, *The Leadership Secrets of Billy Graham* (Grand Rapids: Zondervan, 2005), 118.

CHAPTER 13: NOT ASHAMED OF THE GOSPEL?

1. Lesslie Newbigin, *The Gospel in a Pluralist Society* (Grand Rapids: Eerdmans, 1989), 132.

2. David McCasland, *Oswald Chambers: Abandoned to God* (Grand Rapids: Discovery House Publishers, 1993), 75.

3. Shane Claiborne, "What If Jesus Meant All That Stuff?" *Esquire*, November 18, 2009 http://www.esquire.com/features/best-and-brightest-2009/shane-claiborne-1209#ixzz1DVR9iAgw.

CHAPTER 14: THE HOLY SPIRIT

1. Lauren F. Winner, *Girl Meets God: On the Path to a Spiritual Life* (Chapel Hill, NC: Algonquin Books of Chapel Hill, 2002), 258.

2. For an exploration of the ways Christians speak about the presence

of the Devil in questionable situations, see Trip York, *The Devil Wears Nada: Satan Exposed* (Eugene, OR: Cascade Books, 2011).

3. Brennan Manning, *Abba's Child: The Cry of the Heart for Intimate Belonging*, expanded ed. (Colorado Springs: NavPress, 2002), 60.

4. Brennan Manning, "Brennan Manning Live at Woodcrest," Woodcrest's Columbia Campus, June 15–16, 2007, rebroadcast at Woodcrest's Jefferson City Campus, June 23, 2007, YouTube, accessed August 1, 2013, http://www.youtube.com/watch?v=pQi_IDV2bgM.

FOR FURTHER READING

THIS IS A BOOK FOR those who feel like the "answers" about Christianity have failed them or that they can't overcome lingering doubts or struggles with their faith. I have taken on a somewhat arbitrary list of the most challenging threats to my faith and the faith of those I know. There's no escaping the challenge of keeping each chapter in this book painfully brief while tackling so many topics. To make matters even worse, I have attempted to provide alternative perspectives, thrown wrenches into conventional teachings, and added complexity without necessarily providing clarity if I thought a topic defied simple explanations.

I hope that readers will understand I have only aimed to create more space for dialogue where there is uncertainty, more ground for exploration where there have been dead ends, and more hope for those who doubt. However, as hesitant as I have been to provide neat and tidy resolutions in each chapter, it is important that I help each reader take next steps in their beliefs and practice. To that end, I am providing a series of recommended books for further reading that are tied to each chapter. In the interest of space, I have tried to keep the lists between four and six books for each chapter and the inclusion of a book is not necessarily a personal endorsement. I hope that my starter list will provide readers with some helpful next steps.

PART 1: CHRISTIAN BELIEFS
Chapter 1: Prayer
The Wisdom of the Desert Fathers and Mothers (Paraclete Essentials)
by St. Gregory the Theologian, St. Antony the Great, and St.
Athanasius; edited by Henry L. Carrigan with a foreword by
Jonathan Wilson-Hartgrove
The Cloud of Unknowing by Unknown
Mystically Wired by Ken Wilson
Opening to God: Lectio Divina and Life as Prayer by David G. Benner
With Open Hands by Henri Nouwen
A Praying Life by Paul Miller

Chapter 2: The Bible
Words of Delight by Leland Ryken
*The Bible Made Impossible: Why Biblicism Is Not a Truly Evangelical Reading
of Scripture* by Christian Smith
The Drama of Scripture: Finding Our Place in the Biblical Story by Craig G.
Bartholomew and Michael W. Goheen
Eat This Book: A Conversation in the Art of Spiritual Reading by Eugene H.
Peterson
Four Views on Moving Beyond the Bible to Theology (Counterpoints: Bible
and Theology) by Gary T. Meadors, Walter C. Kaiser Jr., Daniel
M. Doriani, Kevin J. Vanhoozer, William J. Webb, Mark L.
Strauss, Al Wolters, and Christopher J. H. Wright

Chapter 3: Violent Bible Stories
God Behaving Badly by David Lamb
Holy War in the Bible edited by Heath A. Thomas, Jeremy Evans, and
Paul Copan
Is God a Moral Monster? Making Sense of the Old Testament God by Paul
Copan
Show Them No Mercy: Four Views on God and Canaanite Genocide
(Counterpoints: Bible and Theology) by C. S. Cowles , Eugene H.
Merrill, Daniel L. Gard, and Tremper Longman III
Sacred Word, Broken Word: Biblical Authority and the Dark Side of Scripture
by Kenton L. Sparks

Chapter 4: Deliver Us from Evil

Evil and the Justice of God by N. T. Wright

How Long, O Lord? Reflections on Suffering and Evil by D. A. Carson

Walking with God Through Pain and Suffering by Timothy Keller

Exclusion & Embrace: A Theological Exploration of Identity, Otherness, and Reconciliation by Miroslav Volf

Is God to Blame? Beyond Pat Answers to the Problem of Suffering by Gregory A. Boyd

Chapter 5: Hell

Four Views on Hell (Counterpoints: Bible and Theology) by John F. Walvoord, William V. Crockett, Zachary J. Hayes, and Clark H. Pinnock; edited by William Crockett and Stanley N. Gundry

Inventing Hell: Dante, the Bible and Eternal Torment by Jon M. Sweeney

Erasing Hell by Francis Chan and Preston Sprinkle

The Fire That Consumes by William Fudge and Richard Bauckham

The Great Divorce by C. S. Lewis

Chapter 6: Errors in the Bible?

Inspiration and Incarnation by Peter Enns

Scripture and the Authority of God: How to Read the Bible Today by N. T. Wright

Five Views on Biblical Inerrancy (Counterpoints: Bible and Theology) by R. Albert Mohler Jr., Peter Enns, Michael F. Bird, Kevin J. Vanhoozer, and John R. Franke; edited by J. Merrick, Stephen M. Garrett, and Stanley N. Gundry

The Lost World of Scripture: Ancient Literary Culture and Biblical Authority by John H. Walton and D. Brent Sandy

Chapter 7: The Bible and Culture

The Blue Parakeet by Scot McKnight

Coffeehouse Theology: Reflecting on God in Everyday Life by Ed Cyzewski

Misreading Scripture with Western Eyes: Removing Cultural Blinders to Better Understand the Bible by E. Randolph Richards and Brandon J. O'Brien

The Next Evangelicalism: Freeing the Church from Western Cultural Captivity
    by Soong-Chan Rah
Manana: Christian Theology from a Hispanic Perspective by Justo L.
    González

Chapter 8: No Doubt?

Benefit of the Doubt: Breaking the Idol of Certainty by Gregory Boyd
Faith and Other Flat Tires: Searching for God on the Rough Road of Doubt by
    Andrea Palpant Dilley
*Faith Unraveled: How a Girl Who Knew All the Answers Learned to Ask
    Questions* by Rachel Held Evans
Still: Notes on a Mid-Faith Crisis by Lauren F. Winner

Chapter 9: Apocalypse Now?

Reading Revelation Responsibly by Michael J. Gorman
Four Views on the Book of Revelation (Counterpoints: Bible and Theology)
    by Kenneth L. Gentry Jr., Sam Hamstra Jr., C. Marvin Pate, and
    Robert L. Thomas; edited by C. Marvin Pate and Stanley N.
    Gundry
Kingdom Come: The Amillennial Alternative by Sam Storms
*Discipleship on the Edge: An Expository Journey Through the Book of
    Revelation* by Darrell W. Johnson
Revelation for Dummies by Larry Helyer
The Good News of Revelation by Larry Helyer and Ed Cyzewski

PART 2: CHRISTIAN PRACTICES

Chapter 10: Sin Addiction

The Imitation of Christ by Thomas à Kempis
Desiring God by John Piper
The Crucified Life: How To Live Out a Deeper Christian Experience by
    A. W. Tozer
ReCreatable: How God Heals the Brokenness of Life by Kevin Scott
All Is Grace: A Ragamuffin Memoir by Brennan Manning and John Blase

Chapter 11: Money

Christians in an Age of Wealth: A Biblical Theology of Stewardship (Biblical Theology for Life) by Craig L. Blomberg; edited by Jonathan Lunde

Economy of Love: Creating a Community of Enough by Shane Claiborne, Isaac Anderson, and the Relational Tithe network

Free: Spending Your Time and Money on What Matters Most by Mark and Lisa Scandrette

7: An Experimental Mutiny Against Excess by Jen Hatmaker

Chapter 12: Community

When We Were on Fire by Addie Zierman

Disunity in Christ: Uncovering the Hidden Forces that Keep Us Apart by Christena Cleveland

Leaving Church by Barbara Brown Taylor

Dear Church: Letters from a Disillusioned Generation by Sarah Raymond Cunningham

Chapter 13: Not Ashamed of the Gospel?

The Irresistible Revolution by Shane Claiborn

The Celtic Way of Evangelism by George C. Hunter

The Gospel in a Pluralist Society by Lesslie Newbigin

The Open Secret: An Introduction to the Theology of Mission by Lesslie Newbigin

Culture Making: Recovering Our Creative Calling by Andy Crouch

Chapter 14: The Holy Spirit

Spiritual Warfare: A Biblical and Balanced Perspective by Brian Borgman and Rob Ventura

Fresh Wind, Fresh Fire by Jim Cymbala and Dean Merrill

Experiencing the Depths of Jesus Christ by Jeanne Guyon

Flame of Love by Clark Pinnock

Experiencing God by Richard Blackaby and Henry Blackaby

Forgotten God: Reversing Our Tragic Neglect of the Holy Spirit by Francis Chan with Danae Yankoski

ABOUT THE AUTHOR

Ed Cyzewski (MDiv, Biblical Theological Seminary) is the author of *Coffeehouse Theology, Unfollowers: Unlikely Lessons on Faith from the Doubters of Jesus*, and *The Good News of Revelation*. He is a freelance writer, speaker, and blogger who shares his imperfect and sometimes sarcastic thoughts about following Jesus at www.inamirrordimly.com. He contributes to *Red Letter Christians, Church Leaders*, and *Deeper Story*.

Ed lives in Columbus, Ohio, with his wife, Julie, and son, Ethan, where they garden throughout the spring, summer, and fall, and comb the city in search of New York style pizza year round.